Crowood Travel Guides are the essential starting point for a holiday to remember – and they'll be the signpost to enjoyment every step of the way. Easy-to-follow, practical advice, combined with a warmth and enthusiasm for the peoples and cultures of the world, mean that they'll be turned to again and again for direction and inspiration.

Milan

First published in 1991 by
The Crowood Press Ltd
Gipsy Lane, Swindon
Wiltshire SN2 6DQ
© The Crowood Press Ltd. 1991

British Library Cataloguing in Publication Data
Sale, Richard, *1946 –*
    Milan. – (Crowood travel guides)
    1. Italy. Milan. Visitors' guides
    I. Title
    914.0521

    ISBN 1–85223–484–9

Acknowledgements
This book is the product of many stays in Milan spread over a
long period of time. During that time I have benefited from the
knowledge of many of my Italian friends. I would particularly like
to thank Francesco Milone and Monica Neroni for their help and
encouragement. Maria Bernini of the Milanese Tourist Office has
been of considerable help on many occasions, while I have
benefited considerably from the historical knowledge of Maria
Graxia Sempio.
To all those, and everyone else who has helped, thank you.

Photographs by the author
Maps by Taurus Graphics
Typesetting and page layouts by Visual Image
Printed and bound by Times Publishing Group, Singapore

Milan

Crowood Travel Guide

Richard Sale

The Crowood Press

Duomo, Milan

Milan

Contents

Introduction Sandwiched between the high Italian mountains – Alpine mountains to the west, in Aosta and Piedmont, and strikingly beautiful spikes of the Dolomites to the east – and the Apennines, the bone in Italy's leg-shaped south, is the Lombardy Plain. Centuries ago, when ice rather than rivers carved its way between the retaining ridges that now define the shores of the northern lakes, the glaciers brought fertile soil to the plain. The area was endowed with a richness that attracted attention as soon as man decided to sow his food rather than hunt for it.

Those earliest peoples put their settlement in the centre of the Lombardy Plain, the better to police the area. They called it after its position, Mediolanum, the city in the middle. Today we call it Milan.

Italy has always been a land of contrasts, usually between the poorer, agricultural south and the richer, industrialized north. This is still the case today. Despite its lack of natural resources such as fuel and minerals, northern Italy is as rich as any part of Europe, and Milan compares favourably with other cities in the extent and quality of its cultural and economic centres. There are galleries and museums equal to those in many capitals – and Milan also has La Scala. The restaurants are as good as those in favoured culinary centres, the fashion houses are world-famous, and the shops as exclusive as any to be found, with a wide range of goods of excellent style and quality. Even in its sporting achievements the city is noteworthy, its football teams AC Milan and Inter Milan being (some would say) rivalled only by Juventus in the nearby economic rival city of Turin.

To the city explorer Italy usually means the Rome of the Romans or the Renaissance cities of Florence, Venice, Siena or

The campanile of San Gottardo from the roof of the Duomo

Verona, yet Milan has a history that rivals theirs. If its architecture is not as profoundly beautiful, nor characterized by a wholeness that adds to the magnificence, it is because that history has never been frozen in time, Milan having been at the forefront of Italian economic development for centuries.

A visit to Milan is a chance to see elements of all aspects of the history of Italy in one place.

Part One: **Pre-Planning**

**View north-west over the city
from the roof of the Duomo**

How to Get There There are, as always possibilities of travel by road, rail and air.

Travel Documents Italy is in the EEC, so all you need is a British passport. It is also a good idea to carry an E111 form (see Health/First Aid below), and you will also need certain other documents if you arrive in your own car.

By Air Milan is served by two airports. Linate is situated to the east of the city, close to the *Tangentiale autostrada* and only a few minutes from the city centre. Linate is connected to all major European cities, including London by way of both Heathrow and Gatwick. The flight from London takes about 2 hours.

Linate is connected to the city by taxi or by bus. Two buses run. The official Alitalia coach shuttles from airport to Central Station every half-hour and costs 2,200 lire in 1990. Tickets must be bought inside the airport building; they are *not* available on the coach. The second bus is city bus 73 which leaves from the same place – outside and to the left of the central car rental park – and heads for San Babila. This bus is cheaper (800 lire in 1990; tickets from the vending machine at the bus stop, coins only, no change given), but does stop frequently. San Babila has a Metro stop (Line 1, red) for onward travel to the Central Station (change at Duomo on to Line 3, yellow, or at Loreto on to Line 2, green), or Cadorna.

Malpensa is the international airport, situated about 50 kilometres away near the southern tip of Lake Maggiore and close to the Busto Arsizio exit of the A8 (Varese/Sesto Calende) *autostrada*. Connection between Malpensa and Milan is by bus to the Central Station.

Both Linate and Malpensa have excellent car rental facilities, with all the leading European agencies as well as the leading Italian companies.

By Rail Central Station, Milan is connected to all leading European cities, mostly by overnight sleeper trains. There is an information centre at the station, open 7a.m. to 11p.m. every day including Sunday. Central Station is on Metro Lines 2 (green) and 3 (yellow) and is served by a number of buses and trams. There are excellent car rental facilities at the station.

Porta Garibaldi station is connected by motorail link to Paris and Boulogne. From Britain, all-in tickets are available for ferry/train journeys. This service is not cheap, but it is a huge adventure for children and does cut out the long haul across Europe, thus adding several days to your holiday. The trip leaves Boulogne in mid-afternoon, passes Paris in the early evening, goes through the Simplon Tunnel while you are asleep and deposits you for a free (free?) breakfast in Porta Garibaldi at about 6a.m. If you take this route and are leaving Milan on your first day, eat up and be gone. If you wait an hour the Milanese traffic will swallow you whole.

By Car Milan is the best road-connected city in Italy, at the junctions of many *autostrade*.

From France the best way to the city is to go under Mont Blanc, then down the Aosta valley, a fine valley that gets better the further you go up its side valleys, to join the A5. This leads to the A4 and so to Milan.

From Switzerland the very best way is via the Simplon Pass from the Valais to the Ossola valley. Follow the valley to Lake Maggiore and go down its western edge – through Stresa and past the Borromean Islands – to reach the A8 at Sesto Calende.

The alternative way from Switzerland is over the San Bernardino Pass to Bellinzona, then on to Varese and the A8 or, and quicker, linking with the A9 at Ponte Chiasso.

Remember that all *autostrade* are toll roads.

Those travelling to Italy in their own cars should note that they are eligible to receive petrol coupons from the ACI (Italian Automobile Club) offices at the border crossing into the country. The coupon booklet contains vouchers for the *lira* equivalent of about 150 litres of fuel. The booklet offers a discount of about 20 per cent on pump prices and has two other advantages. Firstly a toll card is included for use on automatic *autostrada* booths, amounting to a toll total of 30,000 lire, and secondly possession of the booklet makes the owner a temporary member of ACI so that its emergency services can be called upon. These include free car hire if your car breaks down and will be off the road for more than 12 hours. If you need the service, ring 116.

To obtain the booklet the visitor must be in a foreign car, *not* in a rented Italian car, and must be able to show his car's registration certificate.

The speed limits on Italian roads are as follows:

Engine Capacity	*Autostrada*	All other roads
Cars up to 1099cc Motorcycles 150–349cc	110km/h (68mph)	90 km/h (56mph)
Cars over 1100cc Motorcycles over 350cc	130km/h (80mph)	100 km/h (62mph)
Other vehicles	90 km/h (56mph)	80 km/h (50mph)

In all built-up areas the speed limit is 50 km/h (31mph). It is advisable to keep to these limits; fines are on the spot and non-negotiable.

To drive in Italy you must have a green card insurance certificate, the vehicle's registration certificate, the owner's written permission if the vehicle is not yours, and a translation of your British driving licence (available from British motoring organizations).

Italian traffic regulations require you to wear a seat belt and to carry a warning triangle.

Health and First Aid If your problem is an emergency then telephone for the Red Cross (3883) or for an ambulance (7733).

If your problem is less serious, go to the Fatebenefratelli Hospital (Tel: 63631) where there is a 24-hour emergency service. Look for the sign *Pronto Soccorso*.

Because Italy is a member of the EEC, British visitors are entitled to free health care. To avoid all difficulties with having to pay and then apply for the return of your money, collect a form

E111 from your local DH office before your visit. Possession of this form clears up all problems.

If drugs are prescribed by the hospital they will be dispensed from a pharmacy (*farmacia*), usually identified by a large, flashing green cross. Pharmacies open from 9a.m. to 12.30p.m. and from 3.30p.m. to 7.30p.m. The pharmacy at the Central Station, on the platform floor, is open all the time. Lists of those pharmacies open on Sundays – Sunday opening is on a rota – are available daily in the newspapers *Repubblica* and *Corriere della Sera* or by telephoning 192. When drugs are dispensed a small, non-recoverable tax will be chargeable.

If you require less immediate assistance, English-speaking doctors and dentists are available. Ask at the tourist office for the latest list, together with addresses and telephone numbers. Remember that the tourist office keeps shop hours, so get the list on your first visit. Hopefully you will not need it, but if you do it will probably be in the quiet hours. As an alternative, your hotel reception will probably have the list.

Visitors from countries other than Britain will need to check the validity of their personal health insurance to ensure that they are adequately covered.

Money Banks and change shops (*cambio, wechsel*) are open 8.30a.m. to 1.30p.m. and 3p.m. to 4p.m.. All banks will issue cash against major credit cards, although it is possible that the branch you choose will not have this facility. To be sure, choose one of the bigger branches, usually found at the city centre. Most banks now operate an 'air-lock' door system, that is, one in which there are two doors; the first one you go through needs to be closed behind you before the second will open. Look for the green light or listen for the buzzer before pushing the second door. Of course, you can push if you want to, and in due course the second door will open, but by then everyone in the bank will be looking at you. As a rule, those banks that have the system on the entrance doors also have it on the exit doors.

At the Central Station, there is a change office that is open 7.30a.m. to 10.15p.m. every day.

On the Piazza del Duomo side of the tourist office, No.1 Via Marconi, there is a machine that accepts foreign bank notes and issues Italian lire in exchange. The exchange rate it is offering for

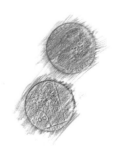

your currency is displayed *before* the exchange is carried out, so you are given the choice of whether or not to go ahead.

Most major credit cards are taken by most hotels, restaurants and shops – look for the stickers in the windows. An exception to this rule is garages (*see* page 21) which will still only, as a rule, take cash.

The Central Station will accept the major credit cards. Counter No.20 also accepts foreign money, but *only* for tickets bought for foreign destinations.

Accommodation

Hotels Until fairly recent times Milan was a businessman's city and the hotels, both in number and type, reflected this. This situation is improving, and the guide to the city's hotels given out by the tourist office is now a fat booklet. The smaller tourist offices at the Central Station and at Linate will also provide this booklet, but none of these offices will book hotels for the visitor. For that service, if you are not doing it for yourself, you need to go to or telephone Hotel Reservation Milan, No.24 Via Palestro (Tel: 706095).

The hotels cover a range from the luxurious (5-star) to the more humble. The price quoted will be for the room not person, (although if you are a single person in a double room you may qualify for a discount), but will not include breakfast (*colazione non incluso*). Should you want breakfast it will be available at a price, but as it will be the same as you can get anywhere, you may prefer to go out each morning to find a new bar to patronize.

5-Star L hotels. There are are only three hotels in this category:

Excelsior Gallia, Piazza Duca d'Aosta, near the Central Station (Tel: 6277). Famous in the 1930s for being visited by princes and other leading world dignitaries.

Palace, Plazza della Repubblica, near the public gardens (Tel: 6336)
Also close to the Central Station. The roof garden offers a fine view of the city.

Principe di Savoia, Piazza della Repubblica (Tel: 6230).
Situated in the same square as the Palace, this hotel offers a check-in service for patrons flying with Alitalia.

5-Star hotels
Duca di Milano, Piazza della Repubblica (Tel: 6284).
Grand Hotel et de Milan, Via Manzoni, 29 (Tel: 801231).
Hilton International, Via Galvani, 12 (Tel: 69831).
Pierre Milano, Via De Amicis, 32 (Tel: 8056221).

4-Star hotels
There are a great number in this category, and your choice between them depends largely upon where you want to stay relative to the city sights. Close to the centre of the city are:

Ascot, Via Lentasio, 3–5 (Tel: 862946).
Cavour, Via Fatebenefratelli, 21 (Tel: 650983).
De La Ville, Via Hoepli, 6 (Tel: 867651).
Jolly President, Largo Augusto, 10 (Tel: 7746).

Closer to the station are:

Auriga, Via Pirelli, 7 (Tel: 6592851).
Bristol, Via Scarlatti, 32 (Tel: 6694141).
Manin, Via Manin, 7–9 (Tel: 6596511).

3-Star hotels
The following are excellent:

Ambrosiano, Via Santa Sofia, 9 (Tel: 5510445).
Bolzano, Via Ruggero Boscovic, 21 (Tel: 6691451).
Centro, Via Broletto, 46 (Tel: 875232).
Club, Via Copernico, 18 (Tel: 606128).
Cristallo, Via Scarlatti, 22 (Tel: 2042101).
Fenice, Corso Buenos Aires, 2 (Tel: 203705).
Manzoni, Via Santo Spirito, 20 (Tel: 705697).
Mini Hotel Aosta, Piazza Duca d'Aosta, 16 (Tel: 6691951).
Puccini, Corso Buenos Aires, 33 (Tel: 220344).
Sempione, Sempione Finocchiaro Aprile, 11 (Tel: 6570323).
Zurigo, Corso Italia, 11a (Tel: 808909).

2-Star hotels

There are fewer in this category, but worth considering are:

Bernina, Via A. Torriani, 27 (Tel: 652185).
Garden, Via Rutilla, 6 (Tel: 55212838).
London, Via Rovello, 3 (Tel: 872988).
Moderno, Via Giuseppe Mazzini, 4 (Tel: 872768).
Rio, Via Mazzini, 8 (Tel: 874114).
Venini, Via Venini, 72 (Tel: 2850480).

As regards 1-Star hotels, it is better to do your own inspecting.

Camping Milan is not convenient for the camper. There are few sites, and they are a long way and difficult to reach. As good as any is the Monza site in the autodrome park (Tel: 039-387771). This is open from May until September inclusive and does, at least, have the advantage of being in delightful surroundings. If you are at the site, then the train can be used to get in and out of Milan, but a car of your own is better unless long periods are to be spent travelling.

The same is true of the other two Milanese sites. AGIP Metanopoli is in Via Emilia (Tel: 5272159), in the San Donato Milanese area of the city. It is reached along the SS9 – leave along Corso Lodi and then follow Via Rogoredo – and is open year-round. The site is not the sylvan delight of the Monza Park.

The final site is Bareffino in Via Corbettina, Bareggio (Tel: 9014417). To reach this you must follow SS11 – leave along Corso Vercelli, then follow Via Rubens and, Via Rembrandt to reach not another painter, but the rather ordinarily-named Via Novara – but beware, it is a long, long way.

Overall, you might feel there is more merit in camping on the side of Lake Maggiore and coming in on the train.

Youth Hostels The Milanese Youth Hostel is at No.2 Via Salmoiraghi, near the San Siro sports complex and the Lotto Metro stop. It is open to anyone with a current IYHF card. If you do not have a card you can register for membership at the hostel. The hostel is open from 7a.m. to 9a.m. and from 5p.m. to midnight. Registration is from 5p.m. to 11p.m. and guests must leave between 7a.m. and 9a.m. on the day of their departure. Breakfast is included in the price.

Stays at the hostels are usually limited to three days, but IYHF international regulations apply.

Getting About

By Car The best advice on driving in the centre is don't. The one-way systems will cause more problems for you than for the locals and the parking situation is worse than in most busy European cities.

If you must drive be very careful where you park. There are several above and underground car pars (identified by a blue P) both in the centre and near the Central Station.

Be careful if you are working on the principle that if there are cars already there then parking is acceptable; they may well know something that you do not. To be safe, look for the sign *Zona Disco*. You may park here for up to 1¹/2 hours, provided you have *a disco orario*, a disc showing the time of your departure that you leave on the dashboard top. Discs are available in kiosks and some bars. Do not post-date your departure time; if you are found out retribution will be swift and officials unimpressed. Note that the same applies to parking fines. You may not be allowed to move your car until you have paid the fine, and being foreign will cut no ice – Milan is full of foreigners.

Beware of any area that displays a sign showing a car being towed away. If you park here then towing away may well be the result. If you return to your car and it is gone, try ringing 77271 and asking for *Rimozione Forzata*. If you are lucky, your car will be in the pound rather than stolen. You then have to get to the pound, pay the parking fine and the considerable sum required to cover the towing.

All Milan's streets are cleaned at least once every fortnight at night. On the previous evening a sign, *Diveto di Sosta*, will be set up. Do not ignore it. The cleaning wagon could come any time between midnight and 6a.m. and if your car is in the way you *will* be fined.

Petrol stations are, in general, open from 7a.m. to 12.30p.m. and 3p.m. to 8p.m., but most close on Sundays. Out of hours, look for signs for 24-hour service. Here there is a pump that accepts 10,000 lire notes.

A Milan tram

**Below
A new Line 3 metre train in
Duomo**

**The sign above all entrances
to the Milan Metro**

By Tram or Bus Milan still has trams, surely one of the most romantic of city conveyances. They are large, orange and silent and some are articulated. Be careful when you are walking – not only will the traffic be coming from the wrong side, but the trams come in all directions and without any noise at all.

None of the vehicles has a ticket seller or is equipped with a ticket vending machine. Buy your ticket from a kiosk or bar. Some shops – especially those at the bigger terminals, Linate, Central Station, and so on – have vending machines, but these usually take exact change only (800 lire in 1990). Alternatively, tickets can be bought from the Metro vending machines which usually take banknotes and give change. If the machine rejects your banknote try again, you may have offered it upside down, or if it was a little crumpled, the machine may have misread it. A ticket can be used for one ride on the Metro and then for as many bus or tram rides as you can fit in.

I say 'fit in', because tickets are valid for 75 minutes rather than for a set number of journeys. When you get on the bus or tram, put your ticket into the punching machine set up inside. This will time-stamp it, and you can keep on using it until a machine rejects it as being out of time. It is illegal to travel without a ticket, with an invalid one or with one that does not have a current time-stamp.

Tickets valid for travel for a full 24-hour period are available from the tourist office. The tourist office will also let you have a map of the current bus and tram routes.

Trams 29 and 30 along the canal circuit (the Viale) run all night, as do the buses on the outer circle road, Nos. 90 and 91. All other buses and trams stop at about midnight.

By Metro Milan's underground system, the *Metropolitan Milanese*, was only begun in the 1960s, so it has not had time as yet to become run-down and unpleasant. In addition the 'sport' of covering the cars with aimless graffiti does not appeal to the young Milanese. The system is, therefore, clean, fast and efficient.

In 1989, there were two lines, with another under construction. In 1990, there were three lines, with the third still being extended. The lines are numbered 1 to 3 (with a logic that does not always apply in such situations), and also identified by colour: Line 1 is red, Line 2 is green, Line 3 is yellow.

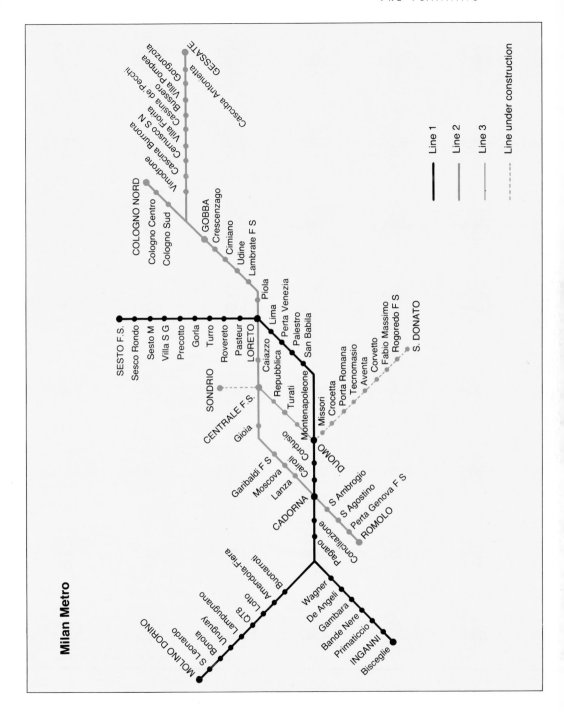

Milan Metro

Line 1
Line 2
Line 3
Line under construction

View south from the roof of the Duomo

Metro stations are identified by a large M on a red square held up above the entrance. As you descend the steps to the station look for the nameplate above the stairway. All metro stations are named and this plate will tell you where you are if you are in any doubt.

When you have bought your ticket (*see* page 22) you will have to use it to get through the barrier on to the platforms. Put it into the time-punch which will free the barrier for you to pass through. If your station is on two lines – few are; Loreto and Cadorna on lines 1 and 2, Duomo and Statione Centrale on Lines 2 and 3 – then check where your platform is, as you may have a very long walk. There is little choice of destination, only of direction. Indeed, if you are travelling within the central area direction is the only thing that is important. However, if you are going further out, for instance, to see the stadium at San Siro on Line 1, then you will need to check the nameplate at the front of the train. That is the only indication of the final destination of the train.

On the train the doors open automatically. There is an emergency stop handle but, as is usually the case, there is a fine for improper use.

Once you are on the train do *not* throw your ticket away. Although you do not need it to get through the barrier at journey's end, you may need it for inspection and will definitely need it if you are changing lines, from Line 1 to Line 2 and so on.

Metro trains start at 6.20a.m. and finish at midnight. To avoid the crush, do not travel between 8a.m. and 9a.m. or between 6p.m. and 7p.m.

By Taxi Milan is provided with a large number of yellow taxis that can be entered at the frequent taxi stands or, if you are lucky, by flagging them down at the roadside. You can call for a taxi on 5353, 6767, 8585 or 8388. Charges are by length of ride, which is a nice idea if the traffic is grim. Milanese taxi drivers are the same as taxi drivers everywhere...

By Foot This is the way to see Milan, but some words of caution are worthwhile.

If you are a woman on your own, it is best to avoid the areas near the castle, Parco Sempione and the Central Station at night. If you must go there, do not carry a cigarette. I do not intend to elaborate.

24

Parco Sempione, although a great place for an evening walk, should really be avoided by all visitors at night as it is the main drug area and, as such, full of undesirables. Piazza Vetra in the Ticinese area is also best avoided.

Milan has a number of beggars, not unusual in these times, but they are not a problem. Groups of small children are more difficult. These gangs – usually about three to six in number – will approach and pester you for money. At first they will beg and plead, but they may also start to pull at you or at your bags. This can be unpleasant; if more than one kid starts on you, who knows where their hands are? If you are approached, do not stop as this places you at a severe disadvantage. Avoid eye contact and do not enter into conversation. If you are tugged, shake yourself free, raise you arm and shout with exaggerated anger. Use of words like *Inglese* and *Polizia* will have a sobering affect, but nothing works as well as a ferocious look and the hint of possible violence.

Food Telling people the best place to eat is fraught with unpleasant possibilities. If you get it wrong, they will never speak to you again; on the day they visit, your favourite restaurant may be undergoing some crisis that means that the soup will be cold, the waiter surly and the bill miscalculated. Overall, I think it is best to settle for the restaurants mentioned in each chapter. Other possibilities will be listed without any comment, except the particular reason that makes it worth mentioning them.

First, some general comments. All restaurants worth frequenting will have a menu posted outside for you to read before entering. To this you will have to add a cover charge (*pane e coperto*, literally 'bread and cover'), for use of the table and for the contents of the bread basket, and possibly a 10 per cent service charge.

The food you eat will depend on where you eat it; Milan, being a major city, can offer you a restaurant specializing in food from just about any country. But it seems ridiculous to come all this way for a Chinese take-away (although it is available if the need comes over you), and the joys of Italian cooking are too many to be extolled here. A few Milanese specialities might be worth mentioning. The best known is *risotto alla Milanese*, a broth with rice and saffron, and there is also *costoletta alla Milanese*, breaded veal cutlet – don't call it Wienerschnitzel or you will be given what can only be termed a 'hard stare'. Another local veal dish is *vitello tonnato*, veal with a tuna fish sauce. Following your main course you might like to try a *panettone*. This cake is made in the usual way, but with lemon rind and sultanas added. It is said that there was once a pastry cook's apprentice called Toni in Milan whose cake dough did not rise. Desperate to hide the fact he added butter, rind, sultanas and sugar. The customers loved it and it became known as *pan de Toni*, 'Tony's cake', in the French that was spoken in Milan at the time. With the resurgence of Italian this became *panatìn*, which became *panettone*. Once a Milan-only cake, *panettone* is now served all over Italy, although the Milanese maintain that they are still the only producers of the real thing.

Of the top-flight restaurants – those that will create a hole of sizeable proportions in your wallet, but will compensate with the gastronomic experience of the trip – most highly rated is *Gualtiero Marchesi*. It is said that you always know you are dealing with a top-quality restaurant when its name is just that of the chef. Marchesi is reckoned to be the best chef in Italy now. His restaurant is at No.9 Via Bonsevin de la Riva (Tel: 741246; reservations essential, closed Sunday and Monday lunchtime), a turning left off Corso XXXII Marzo. This road is a continuation of Corso di Porta Vittoria that passes the Palace of Justice.

Elsewhere, pride of place must go to Savini, the elegant restaurant in the Galleria Vittorio Emanuele, which lies at the heart of Milan's high society. Reservations are usually required here too (Tel: 8058343, closed Sundays).

Another popular spot with theatre-goers is Toulà, in Piazza Paolo Ferrari, off Via Filodrammatici next to La Scala itself. The cuisine here is international rather than Italian, but very good, (Tel: 870302, closed Sundays and Saturdays in June, July and August).

For the rest, it is a question of looking and deciding.

Those wanting a cheaper meal or a faster service will be delighted to find that fast food has reached Milan. The Italian McDonalds are called Italy & Italy and are at No.7 Corso Venezia, No.7 Corso Buenos Aires and in Via Torino at the Carrobio. In addition to the hamburger there is also pasta and pizza.

A slightly more Italian version of fast food, with a more Italian menu, but self-service and with the accent on the fast rather than on the culinary delights, is the Motta/Amico chain. These eating houses are actually very good, so don't be put off by the appearance. Inside, the atmosphere is much less frenetic. There are a large number of houses in the chain, and the ones in the most popular areas for the visitor are at Piazza le Cadorna (Motta Cadorna), No 1. Via Foscolo (Motta Duomo), No. 31 Via Manzoni (Alemagna Manzoni), No. 6 Corso Vittorio Emanuele II (Motta Bari), No. 37 Corso Vittorio Emanuele II (Amico San Babila), Piazza Lima (Amico Buenos Aires) and No. 1 Via Orefici (Amico Orefici).

Finally, do go at least once to the Magic Restaurant in the Galleria wing in Piazza del Duomo, if only to see the astonishing range of things available for take-away eating and drinking.

All over Milan there are bars where you will be able to stop for a few minutes to rest and drink coffee. In most of these – and also in the Magic Restaurant – the procedure is to pay for want you want at the cashier who will issue you with a ticket that you take to the counter. There the 'waiter' will ask you to repeat your order, check your ticket and serve your drink. It usually costs a little extra to sit down, both inside and outside. Traditional Italian coffee (*liscio*) is served in very small cups, is thick and black, usually heaped with sugar by Italians, and lethal in any quantity. There is, apparently, an even stronger version called *ristretto*. If that it true then bars selling it should be required to have a licence.

If you want to prolong enjoyment, life, or both, go for a longer version. *Caffe lungo* is served with hot water, *caffe macchiato* with a little milk. *Cappucino*, vernacularly called *cappucio*, is served with a frothed milk and occasionally topped with chocolate· powder. It is usually drunk at breakfast, and asking for it during the day is the sign of a wimp. You will receive glances that assess your virility. I habitually drink *cappucino* and I know!

Shopping Milan is a paradise for the shopper, merging the best of Italian style, and the best of its specialities – leather and fashion – with the best of international shopping.

The high-class area is bounded by Via Montenapoleone and Via delle Spiga, the latter a pedestrian precinct. Linking the two are Via Borfospresso, Via Santo Spirito and Via Gesù, each with its own high-spots. On the centre side this area is bounded by Corso Vittorio Emanuele II, another pedestrian-only street.

North of here, in an area bounded by Via Fiori Chiari and then leading narrowly northward again to finish in Via Solferino, is the centre for 'young' Milan.

For the 'ordinary' shopper the centres are Corso Buenos Aires which runs from Porta Venezia to the Piazza Loreto; Corso Vercelli which continues Corso Magenta which runs past Santa delle Grazie; and Via Sarpi, to the north of the city, going westward from Porta Garibaldi. Finally, try Centro Commerciale Bonola at No.23 Via Quarenghi, reached directly from the Bonola Metro (Line 1, red, but be sure to take a Molino Dorino train and *not* an Inganni train). This centre has a large number of shops and café/bars.

The named shops are in the Via Montenapoleone area. Here are Krizia, in Via delle Spiga, and Marisa in the same street. Via Montenapoleone has Missoni, Armani, Gucci and Gianni Versace. The leather shops include Mario Valentino, Ferragamo and Sebastian. In Corso Vittorio Emanuele II the shops include Galtrucco and Ragazzeria, Milan's best shop for the fashion-conscious young with three floors of clothes for those aged six to teenage.

Elsewhere there are fine jewellers, antique dealers, and shops that bring the essence of Italian design to furniture, lighting and general living.

Other shops that the Milanese tell me are worth a moment or two of time are Arcando at No. 4 Via Durini, a shoe shop with an 80-year history. All shoes sold here are numbered so that on a later visit you can return to the shop and have them give the pair a look-over. Bianca and Blu at No.53 Via De Amicis sells the fashion clothes of Monica Bolzoni. Traifiori at No. 31 Via Solferino has a range of exclusive knitwear. La Vitrina di Beryl at No. 4 Via Statuto has shoes that make you blink. How long can you go without owning a pair of genuine fifteenth-century reproductions? La Galerie of No. 4 Via Osti will not only sell you all the tools you need to prepare smoked eels and various other delicacies, but give you a course in how to use them. Anaconda at No. 7 Via Bergamini is a modern craft jewellery gallery. Albrizi at No. 8 Bia Bagutta and Legatoria Artistica of No. 5 Via Palermo are exclusive stationery shops, each with a range of hand-crafted items.

For children the range of possibilities is large. Citta del Sole at No. 7 Via Meravigli is one of the best toy shops in the city with a huge stock. Pergioco (No. 1 Via San Prospero) specializes in all things that go into the air, including kites and model planes. Zeppelin (No. 10 Viale Premuda) sells nothing but models, mostly cars and some that are collector's items. Dolls are an Italian favourite. Try La Rinascente for new models, or a visit to Clinica della Bambola at No. 50 Corso di Porta Ticinese, where all manner of spares and additions are available for dolls ancient and modern.

If you are looking for departmental store shopping, you should go to La Rinascente in the Piazza del Duomo. This is Milan's oldest store and still the best of its kind. From the café on the top floor – *Cento Guglie* – there is a good view on the pinnacles of the Duomo.

Elsewhere, Standa is the most common chain store you will pass. Others that offer a similar, budget-line selection are Upim and Coin.

Italian shops use the European sizing system. The comparison of sizes is given below:

High-rise modern Milan (via Santa Sofia)

LADIES
Clothes

British size	6	8	10	12	14	16	18
Eurosize	38	40	42	44	46	48	50

Shoes

British Size	3	4	5	6	7	8	9
Eurosize	36	37	38	39	40	41	42

MEN
Clothes

British Size	34	36	38	40	42	44	46
Eurosize	44	46	48	50	52	54	56

Shoes

British Size	$6^{1}/_{2}$	$7^{1}/_{2}$	$8^{1}/_{2}$	$9^{1}/_{2}$	$10^{1}/_{2}$
Eurosize	39/40	41	42	43	44

Shop hours vary, with some shops – particularly the departmental stores like La Rinascente – staying open all day. For most, however, the hours are 9a.m. to 12.30p.m. and 3.30p.m. to 7p.m.

For a bargain the shopper has a couple of choices. Salvagente at No. 16 Via Bronzetti is a *blocchista*, a shop that sells direct from the warehouse, its lines including many designer labels. Alternatively, try a market. *Bollate* is at Piazza Carlo Marx – take a Ferrovie Nord train from Cadorna to reach the site in about 10 minutes – and is the nearest Milan has to a flea market. It is open on Sunday mornings. *Brera* is in Via Fiori Chiari. This market specializes in old jewellery, glass and ceramics, and is open the third Saturday of each month. *Fiera di Senigallia* in Voia Calatafimi, behind the Basilica of Sant' Eustorgio, is *the* Milanese market.

It is held on Saturdays, has a long history and is renowned for the selling of things that may, or may not, have fallen off the back of a lorry. Be careful with your bag and wallet. *Mercanto dell'Antiquatiato* is held on the last Sunday of each month along the banks of the Naviglio Grande. Occasionally there are 2 kilometres of antiques. *Papiniano* in Viale Papiniano near the Darsena is a huge market with everything from fruit and veg to clothes and furniture. It is held every Tuesday and Saturday. *Piazza Mirabello*, a little way north of the Brera, is full of flowers and fruit, meat and vegetables every Monday and Thursday. *Via Armorari* near Piazza Cordusio holds a market for stamp- and coin-collectors each Sunday morning.

Telephones Almost all the telephones in Milan have now been converted to boxes that take both coins and cards. In all the new ones a red light at the top left of the call box will light if the machine is *out of* service. The machine coin boxes will, as a rule, take 100-, 200- and 500-lire coins as well as *gettone*, tokens made specifically for telephones, available at kiosks, but seen more rarely nowadays. Phone cards are available in 5,000- and 10,000-lire values. The cards are available from kiosks and bars, and also from vending machines in the airports, stations and other large centres. The vending machines take notes and coins. Once you have obtained your card, tear off the top right corner, as indicated, and it is ready for use. Insert it into the slot on the card reader, and wait for the current value to be indicated on the digital screen before dialling. The screen will count the value down for you as your call progresses. If the card runs out during the call you will hear the same warning tone that you hear when you money is running low, but there is a difference – when the card becomes

A typical part of Old Milan (near Ca' Grande)

empty of credit you cannot continue with the call by inserting coins, neither have you the time to insert another card. The call will terminate. If at the end of your call your card remains in credit it will be returned automatically. Be patient; it only *feels* like the machine has eaten it out of spite.

For many, the thought of using a foreign phone system is daunting. In Milan this need not be the case because many of the phone boxes have English instructions. If this still does not allay your fears, you need a SIP office. SIP is the national Italian phone company and in all major towns and cities they have offices in which there are individual booths. Tell the counter staff if you are intending to ring abroad, as not all the booths will do this. When you are given your booth you dial as usual and the price is displayed on a screen in front of you. At the end of the call you pay at the counter. There is a SIP office in the Galleria Vittorio Emanuele open from 8a.m. to 9.30p.m. daily. To find the office if you are going in from the Duomo end, go left at the cross roads.

Similar facilities to those offered by SIP are also available at offices in the Central Station, at platform level, next to the *Gran*

The dial codes from Italy are:
Great Britain 00 44
Canada 00 1
USA 00 1
Australia 00 61
New Zealand 00 64

Bar, from 7a.m. to 7.45p.m. and at the Central Post Office (*Posta Centrale*) at No.4 Via Cordusio, also from 7a.m. to 7.45p.m.

Many bars also show a telephone symbol that indicates that they have a phone you can use. Here you will be able to dial yourself, and the price is registered at the counter where you will pay afterwards. Sometimes, but not always, there will be a booth and a screen to tell you how much the call is costing. Sometimes the phone will just be in the bar and will have no readout. Beware of talking up to the limit of your call; the bar is entitled to add a surcharge for the service so it will cost you more than is registered.

To obtain an international number dial 00. The code for Britain is 44, as from any other country in the world. Remember that when you dial you must leave the 0 off the British STD code. For example, to ring the Italian state Tourist Office in London (Tel: 071 408 1254) from Milan (or anywhere else in Italy), dial 00 44 71 408 1254.

The following are telephone numbers which hopefully you will not need: Police 113; *Carabinieri* 112; fire service 115; ambulance 7733; Red Cross (first aid assistance) 3883; list of pharmacies open on Sundays 192. Other useful services include: 161, the (Italian) speaking clock; 1911, the local weather report; 194, a report on road conditions.

The relief statue of Oldrado da Tressano, Piazza dei Mercanti

Books and Newspapers Most kiosks in Milan, particularly those in the centre, sell English newspapers.

English-language books are available from the English bookshop at No. 12 Via Mascheroni (Metro Conciliazione, Line 1, red) close to Santa Maria delle Grazie, and from the American bookshop on the corner where Via Camperio meets Largo Cairoli, in front of the castle.

Museums

Addresses, Telephone Numbers and Opening Times:

Ambrosiana Art Gallery. 2 Piazza Pio XI Tel: 800146
> Open Sunday–Monday, 9.30a.m.–5p.m. Closed Saturdays and holidays

Leonardo da Vinci's *Last Supper*. Piazza Santa Maria delle Grazie. Tel: 4987588
> Open Monday 9a.m.–1.15p.m., Tuesday–Saturday 9a.m.–1.15p.m. and 2–6.15p.m., Sunday 9a.m.–1.15p.m.

Brera Art Gallery. 28 Via Brera Tel: 808387/862634
  Open Tuesday–Saturday 9a.m.–1p.m., Sunday 9a.m.–2p.m.
  Closed Mondays

Poldi Pezzoli Museum. 12 Via Manzoni Tel: 79488
  Open Tuesday–Friday and Sunday 9.30a.m.–12.30p.m. and
  2.30–6p.m.
  Saturday 9.30a.m.–12.30p.m. and 2.30–7.30p.m. Closed
  Mondays and holidays

Castle Museums. Sforza Castle Tel: 6236
  Open Tuesday–Sunday 9.30a.m.–12.15p.m. and
  2.30–4.15p.m. Closed Mondays and holidays

Modern Art Gallery. Villa Reale Tel: 76002819
  Open Wednesday–Monday 9.30a.m.–12noon and
  2.30–5.30p.m. Closed Tuesdays and holidays

Contemporary Art Museum. Palazzo Reale Tel: 6236
Open Tuesday-Sunday 9.30a.m.–12.15p.m. and 2.30–5.15p.m.
  Closed Monday and holidays

Archaeological Museum. 15 Corso Magenta Tel: 806598
  Open Wednesday-Monday 9.30a.m.–12.15p.m. and 2.30–
  5.15p.m. Closed Tuesdays and holidays

Museum of Milan and Museum of Nautical Art. 6 Via S. Andrea
  Tel: 76004143
  Open Tuesday-Sunday 9.30a.m.–12.15p.m. and
  2.30–5.15p.m. Closed Mondays and holidays

Museum of Contemporary History. 6 Via S. Andrea
  Tel: 76006245
  Open Tuesday-Sunday 9.30a.m.–12.15p.m. and
  2.30–5.30p.m. Closed Mondays and holidays

National Risorgimento Museum. 23 Via Borgonuovo
  Tel: 8693549
  Open Tuesday-Sunday 9.30a.m.–12.15p.m. and
  2.30–5.15p.m. Closed Mondays and holidays

Naval Education Museum. 21 Via S. Vittore
  Tel: 4816885/4817270
  Open Tuesday-Sunday 9.30a.m.–12.20p.m. and
  2.30–5.20p.m. Closed Mondays and holidays

Natural History Museum. 55 Corso Venezia Tel: 6236
  Open Tuesday-Saturday (Nov–Feb) 9.30a.m.–12.30p.m. and
  2–5p.m.; Tuesday-Saturday (Mar–Oct) 9.30a.m.–12.30p.m.

and 2.30–5.30p.m. Sunday 9.30–7p.m. Closed Mondays and holidays

Aquarium. 2 Via Gadio Tel: 872847

Open Tuesday–Sunday 9am–12noon and 2–5p.m. Closed Mondays and holidays

Science and Technology Museum. 21 Via San Vittore Tel: 48010040

Open Tuesday–Sunday 9.30a.m.–4.50p.m. Closed Mondays and holidays

La Scala Theatre Museum. Tel: 8053418

Open Monday–Saturday 9a.m.–12noon and 2–6p.m. Sunday 9.30a.m.–12noon and 2.30–6p.m. (except from October to April inclusive, when closed)

Cathedral Museum. Palazzo Reale Tel: 860358

Open Tuesday–Sunday 9.30a.m.–12.30p.m. and 3–5p.m. Closed Mondays and holidays

Basilica of S. Ambrogio Museum. Tel: 872059

Open Tuesday afternoon–Friday and Sunday 10a.m.–12noon and 3–5p.m. Closed Monday, Tuesday mornings, Saturdays and holidays

Manzoni Museum. 1 Via Morone Tel: 871019

Open Tuesday–Friday 9a.m.–12noon and 2–4p.m. Closed Monday, weekends and holidays

Cinema Museum. Palazzo Dugnani Tel: 6554977

Open Tuesday–Friday 3–6p.m. Closed Mondays, weekends and holidays

Francesco Messina Studio Museum. (Ex church of San Sisto) 10 Via San Sisto Tel: 871036

Open Tuesday, Thursday and weekends 9.30a.m.–12.15p.m. and 2.30–5.30p.m. Closed Mondays, Wednesdays, Fridays and holidays

Spazio Baj, Engravings and Multiple Works. Palazzo Dugnani Tel: 6236

Open Tuesday–Sunday 9.30a.m.–12.15p.m. and 2.30–5.30p.m. Closed Mondays and holidays

Far Eastern Art and Ethnography Museum. 94 Via Mose Bianchi Tel: 4980741

Open Monday–Friday 9a.m.–12noon and 2–6p.m. Closed weekends and holidays and from mid-July to the end of August

Wax Museum. Central Station Tel: 6690495
Open Monday–Sunday 8am–11p.m.

Santa Maria della Passione Museum. 2 Via Vincenzo Bellini
Tel: 791370
Open Monday–Friday 10a.m.–12noon and 3–5p.m. Sunday
3–5p.m. Closed Saturdays and holidays

In addition, Palazzo Bagatti-Valsecchi and Palazzo Sormani will
soon be opened on a permanent basis. Ask at the tourist office
for details.

San Maurizio, with its beautiful frescoes, is usually closed, especially
in summer. When it is open, it is from 3.30p.m.–6p.m. on
weekdays. Ask at the tourist office for details.

Useful addresses

British Consulate, 7 Via San Paolo (Tel: 8693442) (Via San Paolo
runs from Corso Vittorio Emanuele II towards Piazza
Belgioioso.)

Milan Tourist Office, 1 Via Marconi (Tel: 809662) (There is also
a smaller office at the Central Station.)

Hotel Reservation Milano, 24 Via Palestro (Tel: 76006095)

Flight Information for Linate and Malpensa (Tel: 74852200)

Automobile Club Italiano (ACI), 43 Corso Venezia (Tel: 77451)

Italian National Tourist Office in Britain, 1 Princes Street,
London W1R 8AY (Tel: 071 408 1254)

Australian Consulate, 40 Via Turati, (Tel: 6598727)

Canadian Consulate, 19 Via Vittor Pisani, (Tel: 6697451)

US Consulate, 1 Largo Donegani, (Tel: 652841)

Part Two: **Local Colour**

**View south-east over the city
from the roof of the Duomo**

Milan: A Short History The first known inhabitants of Italy lived around a quarter of a million years ago, when the country was mostly inhabited by elephants and rhincerouses. Remains of these first Italians, people who arrived over the land bridge from Africa (as did the exotic animals) have been found not only in the south, but also on the Lombardy Plain, near Verona. These oldest dwellers, hunters of the Paleolithic or Old Stone Age, left few remains of their presence. Not until after the last Ice Age had remodelled the valleys north of the plain, overdeepening them, then damming them with morainic debris to form the great lakes of Maggiore, Como and Garda, did man evolve to the point where he left a permanent imprint on the landscape.

The late Neolithic or New Stone age, and Bronze Age peoples of northern Italy can certainly claim to have left their mark. Visitors to the sites of lake dwellings on Lake Ledro – to the west of the northern tip of Lake Garda – and Lake Varese can still see the remains of the wooden stake piles on which the lake villages were set. Ledro supplies water to a hydro–electric power station and when demand is high, and the water level correspondingly low, some 15,000 wooden stakes emerge from the waters. Equally impressive are the finds exhibited in the museum on Lake Varese's Isolino Virginia. Later, as bronze was replaced by iron, the Golasecca culture arose at the southern end of Lake Maggiore. The culture is named after a village away from the lake, though the better finds have been at Sesto Calende, the town at the end of the lakebound *autostrada* that heads north from Milan.

As the Golasecca culture flourished, elsewhere in Europe the first of the truly great European cultures was rising to the east. The Greeks were not slow in taking to the sea and exporting

Hellenic culture around the Mediterranean basin. Southern Italy, and especially Sicily, had Hellenic cities from an early time. To the north the Celts were arising in central Europe, chiefly expanding northward, but also crossing the Alps to replace the Golasecca culture around the lakes and founding the Gaulish city of Mediolanum, so called because of its position in the centre of the Lombardy plain. Between these two well-known and reasonably well-documented cultures lay one that is, in many ways, still as mysterious now as it was over two thousand years ago.

Herodotus, the Greek, claimed that the Etruscans who held the centre of Italy had migrated from the Middle East, while another Greek, Dionysius of Halicarnassus, argued for a lineage that was home-spun, the Etruscan having evolved from tribes that were contemporaries of the Golasecca people. Today, much the same debate is still taking place. What is known is that this last pre-Roman culture had a vitality and civilization that compared with that of the Greeks. But though their name lives on in the region of Tuscany, the Etruscans actually survived for only a short period; they were expelled from Rome by the Latins and then defeated at the battle of Aricia in 506BC.

This date does not fit well with the founding of Rome by Romulus on 21 April 753BC. That date was 'discovered' by early Roman historians, men who also incorporated the well-known Greek legend that the city was founded by Aeneas after he had escaped from Troy. Romulus and Remus, the wolf children, were, said the Roman historians, the grandchildren of Aeneas. Ironically, the latest historical theorists claim as very likely the idea that the first king of the city of Rome was indeed a Romulus. However, the theory also points out that Etruscan kings are required in the lineage of Roman kings so it is by no means clear that the Romans who emerged out of the Etruscan shadows in the late sixth-century were true descendants of Romulus himself.

At first the Romans consolidated their position in central Italy, moving north only in the third-century BC, when the battle of Mediolanum in 222 BC won them the most important city on the Lombardy Plain. This battle was a bitter, strongly contested affair, the Romans under Claudio Marcello defeating the Gauls who then held the city.

The city's importance derived from its position, right at the centre of the most fertile section of the plain, bounded by the lake peaks to the north, the Po to the south and the lake outflow rivers of the Adda and the Ticino to the east and west respectively. To the west of the Ticino lay the high Alps, and those entering Italy from that direction were funnelled down the Aosta valley towards Mediolanum. To the north the passes through the Alps brought the traveller to Como or Maggiore, and then on down to Mediolanum. Only to the east, was the Lombardy Plain not decisively held by those who held Milan.

So strategic was the city's position that the present inhabitants claim that the dwellers were a people in their own right even by the time of the Roman conquest, and that when Julius Ceasar gave them Roman citizenship they were already famed as an industrious, peaceable, practical people with a legendary ability to confront any misadventures with incredible resources of energy. But then, city dwellers have never been long on modesty.

The rise of Christianity was opposed by the Romans, and most famously by Nero, whose persecutions of the earliest Christians started around 64AD. In all the persecution lasted for about 250 years, being at its height during the reign of Diocletian. Diocletian was Emperor from 284 to 305, a period during which the Empire was under severe threat. To the north the Franks and Lombards threatened, while to the east the Vandals and Huns were carrying out attacks with the violence with which their names are now synonymous. During the years 303–305 Diocletian, convinced that the threat to the Empire was due to the presence of the Christians among the loyal followers, ordered outrageous purges: even his wife and daughter were killed. However, the Christians survived.

After Diocletian had surrendered power there was a time of confusion until Constantine the Great became Emperor in 324. He had already been converted to the new faith, and had, with the Edict of Milan in 313, granted equal status to Christianity. In 391 Theodosius made Christianity the state religion, and died shortly after in Milan, which had become, for a short time, the seat of the imperial court in the western half of the Empire. The city quickly acquired its first Christian bishop, a man now revered as Milan's patron saint, St Ambrose (Sant 'Ambrogio). Ambrose, a native of Treviri, was a severe man, who it was said, would weep bitter tears when confessing a sinner. He laid foundations for Christianity in the city which were to survive the coming of the Barbarians.

St Ambrose died in 397. The Barbarians came in 538. The Goths had been forced out of central Europe by Hun pressure from the east. They settled in the Lombardy Plain, taking the city only after having controlled much of the surrounding area and penetrating deep into southern Italy. The city was devastated and took years to recover. Indeed, full recovery might never have occurred had it not been for the invasion of the area by the Lombards, the people after whom the plain on which the city is set and the region of which it is the capital are named.

There is still uncertainty about the origins of the Lombards – frequently called the Longobards – but it is now generally agreed that they were central European, and probably arrived over the Alps from Hungary. It is known that the Lombard King Alboin brought his army and then his people on to the plain in 568, and that they met with little resistance as the Goths had almost vacated the area by that time. The Lombards had soon occupied an area that extended as far south as Perugia, though not all the way east to the Adriatic coast. The people were pagan, but were converted to Christianity by Theodolinda the daughter of a Bavarian duke who married the Lombard king. For her services to the Christian faith the Pope gave Theodolinda a True Nail. The Lombards incorporated this into an iron crown which was used to crown the kings of Lombardy. Charlemagne was crowned with it, as were the later kings of Italy, including Napoleon. Today it is kept in the cathedral of Monza a little to the north-east of Milan, where it is displayed at certain times.

The Lombard capital was at Pavia, but Milan was rebuilt and slowly regained its former significance. The new rulers were noted for their commercial sense, and the city site was too important to remain undeveloped. It is to the new city rulers that the origins of banking are usually attributed; not for nothing is the home of the London banking community called Lombard Street.

Towards the end of the eighth-century the Lombard kings began to cast a jealous eye on the remnant Roman Empire to the south. The Popes appealed to the Franks for help and they responded by invading Lombardy to administer a sharp lesson. The lesson was not heeded, and when a second call came Charlemagne decided not only to march into Lombardy, but to stay there. He took the Lombard crown and then, in 800, became the first Emperor of the Holy Roman Empire that he formed by annexing central Italy.

Charlemagne was a charismatic man who held his widespread and disparate peoples together as much by force of personality as by force of arms. After his death his empire could barely be sustained by the new rulers (including Charles the Bald and Charles the Fat – is it possible to hold an empire together when the populace is taking the mickey out of you to that extent?) and crumbled away over a period of two centuries.

As the Carolingian Empire was declining, north and central Italy saw the rise of the city states, a progression that was to have perhaps the most profound influence on the history of Europe. The reasons for the rise are many, difficult to unravel with certainty. There was an increase in the population of central and northern Italy which led to a rapid development of agriculture, a rise in general prosperity and a subsequent increase in merchant goods. The coastal ports also saw an increased trade, especially with rich Byzantium. Equally important was the existence of a ruling class willing to put commercial considerations before personal gain. In southern Italy the Normans held the country and imposed a feudal system that stifled mercantile expansion. In the centre and north, and most especially in the north, the new rulers were communes of merchants, men with a vested interest in expanding the local economy, and more concerned with making money than making war. Of all the cities in the north, Milan was the one that expanded most rapidly in the period up to 1100.

Sadly, the idea that friendly trade rivalry could entirely replace warfare was not well founded, and wars sometimes broke out between the city states. Pisa fought Genoa for control of Mediterranean trade, Florence fought Siena for control of the trade route to Rome, and in the Ten Years War (1118-1127), Milan fought the city of Como for control of Lombardy. Como was defeated, but gradually rose again to prominence. It asked for and received the help of the ruler of the Hohenstaufen (Germanic) Empire, Frederik 1, known as Barbarossa ('Red Beard') who crossed the Alps and attacked Milan. In 1158 the city was partially destroyed. In the wake of this defeat Como utterly destroyed the commune from Isola Comacina that held Lake Como for Milan. Comacina never recovered from the beating. Como soon discovered that it was in the nature of winners to enjoy their winnings, as Barbarossa stayed in the north in an attempt to subjugate all the city states. Milan challenged the new ruler and for its troubles was razed to the ground in 1162.

Again Milan rose, this time almost miraculously, and formed the Lombard League of city states. This included both Verona and Venice, as well as Brescia, Bergamo, Novaro and, ironically, Como and was a formidable alliance. In 1176 the League defeated Barbarossa at Legnano to the north-west of Milan.

The relative stability in the north that followed Barbarossa's defeat set the stage for the next step in the rise of the city states. The cities of northern Italy, most importantly Genoa on the Mediterranean coast, Milan in the centre of the Lombardy Plain, dominating the Po valley, and Venice on the Adriatic coast, were on the route of the Crusades. The wealth the Crusades themselves brought was soon eclipsed by the trade wealth that followed in the wake of the construction of the Crusader ships.

By the middle of the thirteenth-century Milan's ruling commune had lost its power, and the city had become one of the first to fall to the *signori*, the city lords. At first Milan was ruled by the della Torre family; Martino della Torre had the revolutionary idea that the city should be governed by the people, with taxes calculated on ability to pay. The experiment did not last, and della Torre rule ended with the family defeat by the Viscontis at the battle of Desio in 1277. The Viscontis, a family that originated in a tiny village, Massino (Visconti), above the western shore of Lake Maggiore, were later themselves replaced by the Sforzas.

In view of the benevolent rule of the communes this might seem to have been retrograde step. In some cases this is true, but Milan fared well, and the Viscontis especially proved to be very able rulers. Gian Galeazzo Visconti was responsible for the construction of a set of canals – here at the lowest point of the Lombardy Plain – and initiated the building of one of the wonders of Italy, the Duomo. He also started the city's silk industry which was to underpin its economy for many years.

By the mid-fourteenth-century Milan was a city of 12,000 houses, 120 bell towers, with 400 bakers, 440 butchers, 180 pubs and more than 1,000 shops. There were 28 doctors, 92 teachers and 1,500 lawyers. The population rose, but was savagely reduced by the Black Death. On its recovery from the Plague the city could claim to be one of the most progressive in Europe, with trade in leather and metal goods, knives and weapons, as well as silk.

As well as prompting a rise in trade, the existence of a new class which found itself with spare time and spare cash at its disposal also heralded an era of unprecedented artistic achievement. This movement has become known as the Renaissance in the English-speaking world, the *Rinascimento* in Italy. By the fifteenth-century, the ducal patronage that supported the Renaissance had provided one of the finest artistic climates ever to have occurred in world history. At one time Leonardo, Michaelangelo, Raphael and Titian were all working simultaneously in northern Italy. Some of their masterpieces were housed in buildings designed by their contemporary Palladio.

In Milan the recipient of the patronage was Leonardo da Vinci, the ultimate Renaissance man, inventor of the submarine, the helicopter and the contact lens, painter of the *Mona Lisa* and the *Last Supper*. The latter survived the bombings of World War II better than it survived the ravages of time after Leonardo's highly original method of fresco working failed to live up to its inventor's hopes, but it still remains one of the masterpieces of Renaissance art.

The sixteenth-century started with a power struggle in Europe between the Holy Roman Empire and France, a battle that continued for many decades, with the conflict chiefly centring around Milan. The city's importance was owing to the new Emperor, Charles Habsburg, succeeding his grandfather in 1519 to become Charles V. The House of Habsburg held Germany and Spain, and Milan and the eastern end of Lombardy held the key to a potential land bridge between the two – a bridge desired by Charles and feared by France. On the domestic front the Archbishop of Milan in the mid-sixteenth-century was St Charles (San Carlo) Borromeo, born in Arona Castle on the western shore of Lake Maggiore in 1538. Charles was a cardinal at 22 and archbishop at 26, a spectacular rise to prominence, (although probably helped by his uncle being Pope Plus IV). Charles did a great deal to assist the lot of the Lombardian peasantry whose lives had fared badly during the conflicts that succeeded the Renaissance. This assistance inevitably spilled over as an increase in general prosperity for the ordinary Milanese city dweller. On the debit side Charles was legendary for his rooting out of heretics, and the area was frequently lit up by the glow of those perishing at the stake. After his death miracles were attributed to him and he was made a saint; there were many who maintained that he was too ugly to be anything else. Those who would like to check the validity of this view can see his portrait in the church at Arona or, more spectacularly, visit the colossal statue to him that stands a little to the north of the town. The statue, nearly 24 metres high on a plinth itself 12 metres high, has the large ears and nose that appeared to have been such prominent features of the great man.

Ultimately, the fragmentary nature of the Habsburg empire led to its fall, leaving the Spanish in control of Italy, a position they would maintain until the early part of the eighteenth-century when they lost it with the War of the Spanish Succession. The last Spanish governor left Milan on 29 September 1706, to be replaced on the following day by Austrian and Piedmontian troops. The Milanese cheered until they were hoarse. The change of ruler was formalized by the Peace of Utrecht in 1713 which gave Italy to the Austrian Habsburgs.

Initially the city responded well to the change of ruler, and its economic fortunes improved. In 1769 the Golden Madonna, unofficial symbol of the city, was placed on the highest spire of the Duomo. There followed a burst of building that radically changed the face of the city. Some of these buildings were galleries and libraries, and the city underwent a mini-Renaissance in the wake of the Spanish departure.

Milan became the first city in which all the houses had glass in their windows rather than draped waxed canvas, a material that was virtually opaque and frequently filthy. At the same time most of the streets of the centre were cobbled. Part of this reconstruction had important implications for the rest of Europe, each street being given an official name and every house a civic number. The year after this, street lighting was

45

introduced using oil lamps on pillars; there was a drastic reduction in the number of muggings at night, a plague of city life in the late eighteenth-century.

In 1788 La Scala was opened. It was immediately described, by no less a personage than Maria Theresa, the hand of the Habsburgs in Milan, as the most beautiful theatre in the world, – an ambitious claim. At the time it was poorly lit, with no heating, and it was soon being equally definitely described as 'dirty'. The stages were used as dining rooms, with the orchestra pit a bedlam of shrieking servants. In the foyer a gambling room operated, legend having it that the young Alessandro Manzoni was discovered there by Vincenzo Monti and beaten so hard by him that he never gambled again. Yet despite all this La Scala soon became the focal point of Milan society and culture. Later, when there was a resurgence of Italian nationalism, La Scala became an even more potent symbol to the Milanese. The rise in nationalistic fervour coincided with the rise in standing of Verdi, whose initials spelled *Vittorio Emanuele, Re d'Italia* an anthem for the return of the monarchy and a united Italy. Everywhere the city rang to cries of *Viva VERDI*, a call which did neither the composer nor the opera house any harm at all.

As the eighteenth-century came to a close, the rise of Napoleon following the French Revolution resulted in war between France and Austria, with the French army marching across the Alps to invade the Austrian territories of Piedmont and Lombardy. In a series of bloody encounters in 1796 Napoleon threw back the Austrian, liberating the Italians – again – and created several new republics, one of which, the Cisalpine Republic, had Milan as its capital. Having secured the area, Napoleon went off to fight elsewhere. The Austrians returned in his absence, and were assisted in their reconquest by the Russians and the Italians themselves who were never more happy, it seems, than when they were assisting one despot to overthrow another. In 1800 Napoleon returned, winning the decisive battle of Marengo to overthrow the Austrians yet again. This time, in an effort to produce a lasting solution to the Italian question, Napoleon created a kingdom of Italy, making Milan its capital and having himself crowned with Monza's iron crown. It was a short-lived kingdom. Napoleon

Opposite
View along Corso Vittorio
Emanuele II from the roof of
the Duomo

47

went on to meet his Waterloo, and the Congress of Vienna, in 1815, reinstated the Austrians in Lombardy.

There is a dispute among historians about whether the Napoleonic episode, with its creation of an Italian state by name, was a benefit or a hindrance to the Italian nationalism which had begun to be voiced along with the cries of *Viva Verdi*. The facts are that within a decade of the Vienna Congress, nationalism was gathering furious pace. In 1842 a new newspaper was launched in Turin. It was called *Il Risorgimento*, the 'the reawakening', and it gave its name almost as a battlecry to the forces of unification.

The opportunity for unification came in 1859 when the Kingdom of Sardinia – the island of Sardinia itself, together with Piedmont, Savoy and territory around Nice – sided with France in a war against Austria. The campaign was supported by a disparate band of politically astute Italians who loyally buried their differences in order to fight for unity: Carlo Alberto, the Piedmontian king of Sardinia, and Camillo de Cavour, his Prime Minister, Giuseppe Mazzini, an anti-monarchist from Genoa, and Guiseppe Garibaldi, a romantic, enigmatic guerilla leader born in Nice.

The war for independence was fought on several fronts. In the north Lombardy was liberated after the bloody but decisive battles of Magenta (mid-way between Milan and Novara) and Solferino (to the east of Milan, near the southern tip of Lake Garda) in 1859. Following this northern campaign, in which Garibaldi commanded a force, the new Italy ceded both Savoy and Nice to its French allies. Appalled by the loss of his native town, Garibaldi left the army of Piedmont, but did not leave behind the cause of unification, sailing to Sicily with his famous 'Thousand'. On the island Mazzini had already prepared the ground for an uprising against the Kingdom of the Two Sicilies which controlled the island and the mainland province of Reggio-Calabria. Garibaldi defeated the Neapolitan army and added the territory to the new Italy. Just before this famous victory the army of the north succeeded in annexing Tuscany. In 1866 the Austrians were thrown out of Venetia, and in 1870 the last remaining territory of the Papal states was annexed. The new Italy was complete; almost.

Peace within the new boundaries allowed Milan to make up for the time lost during the bloody years of Napoleon's campaigns and the *Risorgimento*. The city grew to 250,000 people and became a centre for the paper industry. In line with the rest of Europe, Italy invested in the railways, and soon Milan was connected to Zurich, Paris, Berlin and Vienna, as well as the more local commercial centres of Genoa, Venice, Rome and Naples. The main central station was completed in 1864 in grand, if angular, style. At the same time, or shortly after, there was other building in the grand style that best reflected the new confidence of both the city and the country – the main Duomo square was rearranged, and the Galleria built.

Towards the end of the nineteenth-century there was general unrest in Italy, a situation brought about by a number of oddly conflicting factors. In Africa the Italian army set about building an empire, encouraged by the British, but found that the natives of Somalia and Ethiopia (then Abyssinia) were less enamoured of the idea than were their new masters. On two separate occasions they slaughtered large number of Italian troops, and these events caused civil unrest at home. Unrest was also being caused by a rise in socialism, and the odd situation arose where socialists and expansionists were united in common disagreement with the government. In Milan there were riots which, in 1898, resulted in the army being ordered to fire on the crowd. Almost 100 Milanese died. In 1900 the king, Umberto, was assassinated. He was quickly replaced by his son, Vittorio Emanuele III, who appointed Giovanni Giolitti as Prime Minister. Giolitti was an astute politician who satisfied the socialist leanings of the populace with a series of enlightened reforms, but who failed to do anything to control the corruption of those in power. Indeed he almost perfected the system to his own advantage, sowing the seed for the rise of Fascism at the same time by installing in the population the notion that the business or politics was none of their business and that they should shrug their shoulders in a resigned way and let it continue. Giolitti also harnessed the nationalist fervour that still existed by embarking on a colonial war for Libya. The war was costly and pointless. Giolitti lost power, and his government was pilloried by the socialists who whipped up public opinion in their newspaper, *Avanti*, edited by a young man with a future, Benito Mussolini.

Before Mussolini was able to take his chance, Italy was drawn into World War I. At first she remained neutral, but in 1915 threw in her lot with the allies and declared war on Austria. The Italians fought with great courage, especially in 1917 when they stopped a superior axis force that threatened to take over the whole of the northern part of the country. Sadly though, when the peace came it was not so glorious, and the Treaty of Versailles in 1919 gave the Italians little of the territory they had been told to expect in whispered conversation in secret corridors while the war was in progress. Italy got the south Tyrol and Istria – although not the town of Fiume (modern Rijeka) – but little else of consequence. The Italians were outraged. D'Annuzio led a group of men to occupy Fiume for the Italians, lording over the city for almost a year before being ousted by the wartime Allies.

The occupation did nothing except to fuel the sense of outrage the Italians felt about their treatment at the hands of the older powers. The outbreak of nationalist fervour that followed these events was the impetus for the meteoric rise of Mussolini's new party, the Fascists, formed in Milan in 1919 with a grand total of 145 men. The Fascists claimed that their name derived from the *fasces*, bundles of rods carried as a symbol of power by victors of the Roman Empire. In reality this was a later touch, added to increase authenticity when the rod bundle was adopted as the party's emblem. In truth the name was just derived from the Sicilian (*fasci*) for a group. Mussolini had some ominously persuasive sayings – 'who has steel has bread' was one of the most popular – but failed miserably at his first attempt to gain legal power in 1920. Only when his party took to wearing black shirts, and 'disrupting' meetings of the opposition in order to save Italy from them, was there any ground-swell of popularity. In elections in 1921 Mussolini won a seat in Milan, and his party gained 35 of 535 seats in the country.

In 1922 the Fascists marched on Rome and forced the king to accept Mussolini as Prime Minister. Mussolini himself did not take part in the march, but waited at Milan for the call to power. It came on 28 October, and *Il Duce* took an overnight train to Rome to accept the king's offer on the following day. In 1924 Mussolini survived a personal crisis when he was accused of colluding in the murder of Giacomo Matteotti, an opposition leader, and finally became head of state in 1925 when the Fascists banned all other parties.

The rise of Fascism was welcomed at the time, not only by the Italians but by many others, including the British Prime Minister, Baldwin, and Winston Churchill, who probably saw in the movement a bulwark against Bolshevism. In Italy the regime worked, at least in the early stages. During the early 1920s the Italian economy expanded dramatically, and by 1931 Milan had more than a million inhabitants, a formidable industrial power base. The city now realized an old dream by recovering the canals. The problem was that Fascism was a movement with a hollow centre. Mussolini harangued his people long and often, peppering his speeches with slogans like 'it is better to be a lion for a year than a sheep for a hundred years'. It was rousing stuff, but what did it actually mean?

Ultimately to support his power Mussolini was required to invent goals. It is a popular story that the Fascists did at least get the trains to run on time, and had that been all things might have turned out for the better, but the Duce also evolved the theory of *Italia Irredenta*, 'Unrecovered Italy'. In support of this the trains were filled with young Italians, dispatched to liberate Abyssinia, to help Franco in Spain and to capture Albania. The axis formed with Hitler's Germany in 1936 became the Pact of Steel in 1939. At first Mussolini was the senior partner, a position which gave him the feeling of power he clearly relished. Too rapidly, however, Mussolini became the junior partner, carrying out the Führer's personal wishes and dragging Italy into a disastrous war when it had neither the industrial base of Germany, nor Hitler's personal enthusiasm for total war.

Italy entered the war in 1940. It went badly almost from the start, the Italian soldiery having as their only motivation for fighting the increase of Hitler's empire. There was little glory for Italy in dying on the Russian front, as so many did in 1942. By 1943, when the Allies invaded Sicily, the Italians had had their fill of Fascism and changed sides, although the removal of the Germans from their country was a long and bloody business. Hitler had Mussolini rescued from Rome and installed as head of the Republic of Salò, a small, relatively insignificant town on the western shores of Lake Garda, but it was a temporary measure.

51

Typical open air art exhibition – this one is in Via Francesco Sforza

Pressed by Hitler, Mussolini gave speeches of encouragement to the still-occupied Italians of Milan, but his heart was no longer in it. In April 1945, as the partisans and Allies were freeing the last parts of northern Italy, Mussolini was smuggled out of Milan by the Germans. He was driven north along the edge of Lake Como. At Dongo the motor column was halted and Mussolini, his mistress Clara Petacci and other leading Fascists were hauled out. All but Mussolini and Clara were executed in Dongo; those two were taken off towards Milan. They only reached Azzano, where a partisan leader, fearful of the kind of publicity the Italians would receive if they handed over their ex-Duce to the Allies, had them put up against a wall and shot. The bodies of the leaders were taken to Milan where they were hung upside down from a girder in front of a petrol station in Piazza Loreto.

Following the end of the war the king, Vittorio Emanuele III, abdicated and a national referendum abolished the monarchy in favour of a republic, with the new king, Umberto II, going into

exile. In 1949 Italy became a member of NATO and later a founding member of the EEC whose charter was established in the Treaty of Rome.

Milan did not survive the war intact. Allied bombings in 1943 devastated the city, and the light from the fires was visible for many miles out across the plain. Piazza Duomo suffered terribly, although the cathedral itself remained largely intact. The Galleria was shattered, La Scala gutted. the Ambrosiana was destroyed, the Natural History Museum reduced to a pile of ashes. The refectory that housed Leonardo's *Last Supper* had suffered almost complete destruction, yet the fresco itself survived, almost, it seemed, by a miracle.

Official data suggests that 80 per cent of Milanese houses were struck by bombs or incendries, with about 15 per cent destroyed and a further 20 per cent damaged beyond repair. Almost all the city's factories were gone; its tramway system, the main artery for transport, had suffered 70 per cent total damage. There was severe

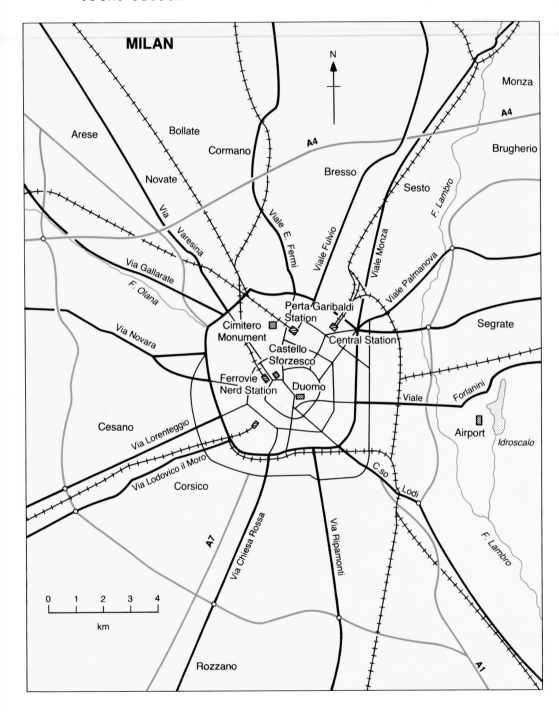

MILAN

N

Monza

A4

Brugherio

Arese

Bollate

Cormano

Bresso

Sesto

Novate

Via Varesina

Viale E. Fermi

Viale Fulvio

Viale Monza

Viale Palmanova

F. Lambro

Via Gallarate

F. Olana

Segrate

Via Novara

Cimitero Monument

Perta Garibaldi Station

Central Station

Castello Sforzesco

Ferrovie Nerd Station

Duomo

Viale

Forlanini

Cesano

Via Lorenteggio

Airport

Idroscalo

Via Lodovico il Moro

C.so Lodi

F. Lambro

Corsico

A7

Via Chiesa Rossa

Via Ripamonti

0 1 2 3 4

km

Rozzano

A1

disruption to the gas, water and electricity supplies; the schools had all but disappeared.

The Milanese turned to reconstruction with a will, deciding that everything that could be returned to an 'as before' condition should be. In ten years the city had risen, phoenix-like, from the ashes; in five more it was leader in the Italian economic miracle. In the 1970s and 1980s Milan had changed again, in an equally remarkable fashion, passing early into the age of electronics and computers to become the undoubted economic capital of Italy.

Layout of Milan Like most other cities with a long history, Milan has evolved as a series of concentric rings. It is believed that the extremes of the original Gallic town were Piazza del Duomo and Via Andegari, which lies close to the Poldi-Pezzoli Museum some 600 metres to the north. In the old language *andegari* meant hawthorn, and a bush of that type probably at one time marked the external borders of the city of Mediolanum, although little or nothing is known of that first town.

The Roman city was larger, and more ordered, lying within a wall erected by the Emperor Augustus in the first-century AD. Parts of the Augustinan wall have been found in the streets of the inner city, enough to trace the route of the old walls along Via Agnello, that runs into the north-east corner of Piazza del Duomo, Via Paolo de Cannobio, Via Brisa, Via Cusani and Via Filodrammatici, as well as several of the roads in between these. The enclosed area is roughly triangular, not at all the square you might imagine, and is surprisingly big, about 1km (over half a mile) across its longest axis. Within these walls (and contemporary writing says they were formidable), the city remained for two centuries. Then in the third-century AD, at the time of the Emperor Maximian, the city outgrew its walls, and new walls were added to allow an extension to the north-east and the west. The old wall was not removed, but fell into disrepair, disappearing over the years. If other cities are a guide to Milan then it also served as a useful quarry for the inhabitants.

Enough of the old wall existed in the fourth-century for the poet Ausonio to speak of the 'town of two walls'. It would seem that the old wall did not finally disappear altogether until the eighth-century, well after the city had been devastated by the Goths.

The next bursts of building coincided with the city's conflict with Barbarossa, when a wide and deep ditch was dug about 300 metres outside the Maximian wall. The resulting circular defence was not complete, its traceable line ending where the castle now stands. This was because earth from these defensive earthworks, or *terraggi*, was thrown up to form the city's first fortress. It was not until the first half of the fourteenth-century that Azzone Visconti reinforced the structure with walls.

When the city decided to construct its canal system the defences of the *terraggi* were flattened and a circular waterway – with obvious defensive uses – was constructed just outside it. The line of this waterway is readily discernible on maps and photographs as it follows a circular path from the castle along the streets of Pontaccio, Fatebenefratelli, Senato, San Damiano, Visconti di Modrone, Sforza Francesco, Santa Sofia, Molino delle Armi, de Amicis and Carducci.

Although the central waterway was a spectacular construction, the most remarkable work was the Martesana canal that linked the city's internal waterway system with the river Adda. The canal can be readily followed from the river near Canonica d'Adda through to the Central Station where it peters out beside Via Tirano. Elsewhere, the most evocative waterways lie to the south of the city centre where morning mist over the water adds a wonderful dimension to views around the Porta Ticinese.

The circular waterway remained until the early nineteenth-century when it was filled and converted into a road. Today, where once silent, slow barges made their way along flat, calm water, mornings offer a view of a noisy metal river.

Even the canals were not the last protective ring around the city, the ramparts or Spanish walls being built – between 1549 and 1561 – in a circle a few metres outside the waterway circle. The name 'Spanish walls' (*mura Spagnole* or *bastione*) commemorates the Spanish governor of Milan, Ferrante Gonzaga, who had the walls built to plans by an Italian architect, Giuntallodi. The position of these ramparts is also visible on street maps, the walls running along the line of Corso di Porta Vercellina, then between the gates of Porta Ticinese, Porta Romana, Porta Venezia, Porta Nuova and Porta Garibaldi. Again the castle formed the focal point of the walls. Here, however, there is a difference because the canal ring has formed two parallel roadways – for instance, near Porta Romana the line is given by the parallel streets of Regina Margherita and Montenero. The names are interesting too, the city fathers deciding to name much of the outside ring after sites made legendary by exploits of Italian soldiers in World War 1 – Montenero, Premuda, Monte Grappa, and so on – while many of the inner ring streets were named after women famous in the history of the city – Regina Margherita, Beatrice d'Este, Bianca Maria, and so on.

Following the rebuilding after World War II one last ring was created, not set on the line of an ancient set of bulwarks, but designed with the future in mind. This wide boulevard forms the impressive (some would say interminable) Viale delle Regioni, which winds its way for miles through what were once the Milanese suburbs, and which today form an area close to the heart of metropolitan Milan.

Structure of the Book Within these great defensive rings, particularly the outer ones, there is too much to see in one go; as with all cities Milan can comfortably fill almost any amount of the inquisitive visitor's time. The best way is to ignore the ring structure and explore the city in chunks that are easy on the feet and brain, keeping in mind your position with respect to the old city plans where it is relevant.

This book covers six journeys within the city, all of them – with a few minor exceptions – staying within the boundary of the old city walls. There is much to see, and hopefully the detailed instructions and maps will prevent you from getting lost. The city of Milan has also thoughtfully provided virtually all of its better buildings with name plates to help the visitor. These are bright yellow and usually mounted on poles outside the entrance to the building. The plate has the symbol of the city, a stylized version of the Visconti family's snake/saracen symbol, together with the building's name, its age (either as a date for construction or as a century if the true date is not know or irrelevant), and the name of the architect if known.

Each of the journeys has been chosen to visit one of more of the city's parks or quiet areas where the visitor can pause and take stock. No attempt has been made to choose worthwhile bars that can be visited for a coffe break *en route*. Milan is full of excellent coffee shops and it is better for the visitor to choose what appears to be best for him, her or them. The same argument could readily be made for restaurants, but there is a difference. If you do not like a coffee house you have lost only the price of a cup of coffee and a few minutes of your time. If the restaurant is a disaster, the price, both in money and time, is that much higher. For this reason I have made a suggestion for eating on each journey. There is also a section (pages 25-27) giving restaurants that are thought excellent, either by me or by trusted friends.

After the six inner-city journeys there is information on those parts of the far-flung city that might be of interest, together with transport suggestions for reaching them. There is also a short section on the area around Milan, or, at least, those parts of it that can be comfortably reached in a day's road or rail travel.

I hope you find a stay in Milan as rewarding as I always have.

Climate The average monthly temperatures in the city during the year are given below:

January	4°C (40°F)
February	6°C (44°F)
March	11°C (52°F)
April	17°C (62°F)
May	22°C (72°F)
June	24°C (76°F)
July	27°C (80°F)
August	24°C (76°F)
September	22°C (72°F)
October	18°C (64°F)
November	11°C (52°F)
December	6°C (44°F)

The normal summer day will be hot and sticky, the city haze holding in some moisture. Bright clear days when the Alps can be seen are rare, (and the more pleasurable for being so), and if you want such days you had better come in spring or autumn when the heat haze is reduced. Those who have viewed the Lombardy Plain from a distance will know that even on clear days Milan has its own atmosphere, the way that other cities do, although, in fairness, it is very much less than many others, despite its low-lying position.

In winter, snow is rare, and the normal day is damp and cold. Indeed, fog can overwhelm the city on as many as 15 days in a winter month, while that will happen on only about 2 days a month in summer. This incidence of fog is the reason that Linate has such a notorious reputation for re-routed flights.

Milan is usually still, the wind rarely sweeping full tilt across the Plain. Statistics show that the average wind speed is around 6 knots (about 7mph or 11kph), and that the wind blows from the south-west.

Those wanting to avoid rain should avoid winter trips, in December in particular, but, as is usually the case, such generalizations will almost certainly not apply to your trip!

Public Holidays

1 January
6 January (Epiphany)
Easter Sunday and Monday
25 April (Liberation day, 1945)
1 May
15 August (Ferragosto)
1 November (All Saints)
7 December (Sant' Ambrogio)
Christmas Day and Boxing Day

Part Three: **Milan**

**Galleria Vittorio Emanuele
from Piazza del Duomo**

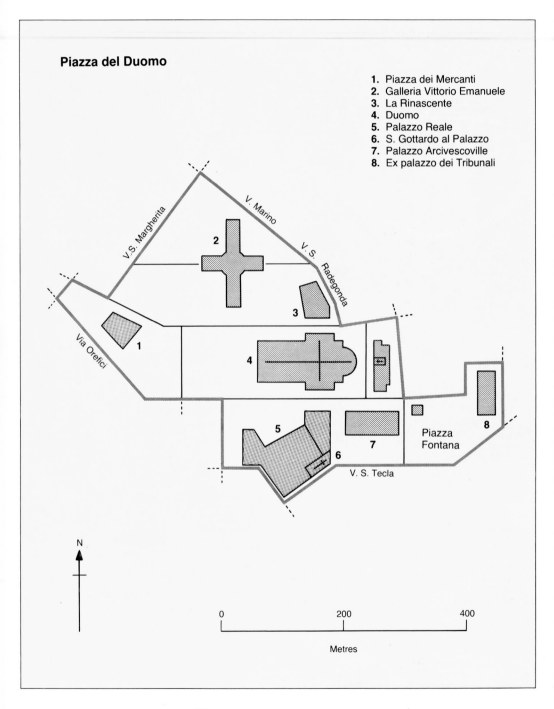

Piazza del Duomo

1. Piazza dei Mercanti
2. Galleria Vittorio Emanuele
3. La Rinascente
4. Duomo
5. Palazzo Reale
6. S. Gottardo al Palazzo
7. Palazzo Arcivescoville
8. Ex palazzo dei Tribunali

V.S. Margherita

V. Marino

V. S. Radegonda

Via Orefici

Piazza Fontana

V. S. Tecla

N

0   200   400

Metres

Piazza del Duomo It would be barely conceivable to start a journey of exploration through Milan other than in the Piazza del Duomo. As with all big cities, to the first-time visitor Milan is too big, too noisy, too fast, its people too busy, in too much of a hurry. But whether you are here for the first or merely the latest time, as you enter the square – better still, as you emerge into it, blinking away the bright Milanese light as you climb up out of the Metro – there can be no doubting its magical ability to conjure a timeless moment of calm from out of the bustle. The reasons for this are many – the sheer size of the square, the three surrounding sides that are dominated by elegant *palazzo* walls that add a solidity that speaks of permanence, but mostly the Duomo, the cathedral, whose façade is among the most beautiful in the world; in the sun, its marble is eye-achingly white.

The Duomo Only St Peter's in the Vatican and Seville Cathedral are bigger than Milan's Duomo. It is 157 metres long, 92 metres across at its widest, the façade is 68 metres wide, the top of the golden Madonna's statue (*Il Madonnina*) is 108 metres

Piazza del Duomo

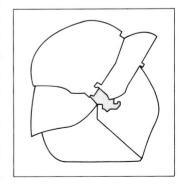

high, and the whole cathedral has been calculated to weigh in excess of 325,000 tons. There are nearly 3,200 statues of all sizes, varying from the very small to the very large; the building can seat almost 40,000 people. Finally, someone once calculated that if the pillars and spires were stood one on top of the other they would be 5,300 metres high. Mont Blanc is 4,808 metres high.

In Roman Mediolanum there was a temple, probably to Minerva, where the cathedral now stands. This was replaced in the fourth-century by a church built by Sant' Ambrogio and dedicated, at a later time, to St Tecla. Near the site, perhaps under what is now the Palazzo Arcivescovile, was the city's first Bishop's Palace, called the *Domus*, from which the name *Duomo* derives. Later, a second church was built behind Sant' Ambrogio's church, making the site one of the focal points for Milanese religious life.

In the mid-fourteenth-century the Archbishop of Milan, Antonio da Saluzzo, spurred on by the population, asked Gian Galeazzo Visconti, Duke of Milan, to support the building of a cathedral on the site of the two old churches. The Duke gave his blessing to the project, placing his own marble quarries at Candoglia in the Ossola valley at the disposal of the builders. The official date of the starting is 1387, as shown on a plaque set in the wall at the south-west corner of the building: *El Principio il Domo di Milano fu nel Anno 1386.* However, this tablet was only set in the wall in 1456, and is in conflict with an account written about events on 17 September 1387. Then a group of local armourers assembled in the square, were blessed at a makeshift altar and turned the first shovelful of earth on the foundations of the new building. Before the end of the month the armourers had been replaced by drapers, bootmakers, butchers, bakers and millers. All these workers gave their time and labour freely, their efforts being supported by other citizens who hauled stone and earth at every available opportunity. The stone came from Candoglia by water, each stone being inscribed AUF, *ad usum fabricae*, 'for building use', a sign that freed the stone of all city taxes. Ironically, later *auf* became a local expression for a long wait, or working for nothing.

Certainly those who were in the square in 1387 hoping to see the completion of the Duomo would have had to wait a long time, far longer than the span of a human life. Not until 1774 was the Madonnina added to the top spire, and even then the façade

Opposite
The roof of the Duomo

was not finished. Over the centuries the best Italian architects, Solari, Amadeo, Pelligrino Tibaldi (known as *Il Pellegrini*) and Richini, worked on the building, although the façade was actually finished by Carlo Amati, the final stage being completed after many years of inactivity, and only after Napoleon took an interest in the building.

Externally the most dominating part of the Duomo is the façade, although technically the best is the apse at the furthest end of the Square, which is best seen from either Corso Vittorio Emanuele II or the Piazza Fontana. The apse is widely believed to represent the peak of Gothic architecture in Italy and was completed at a time when many of the architects working on the project had been brought in from Germany.

The façade, as well as the rest of the outside, is of Candoglia marble, a white stone with a pink tinge and blue veins that could not have been bettered as a choice for so ornate a structure. The façade is pierced by five doorways filled with bronze doors, some of which are remarkably new for so ancient a building. The central doors are by Ludovico Pogliaghi and were finished at the end of the nineteenth-century; the door panels represent episodes in the life of the Virgin, the 'light' being the Coronation. Those interested in seeing more of the sculptor's work can visit a museum to him in the village of Sacre Monte, just north of Varese, where he died in 1950. That museum includes the plaster casts of the doors. The extreme left doors date from 1948, the work of Arrigo Menerbi, showing the tribulations of early Christians. The next doors are by Giannino Castiglioni, completed in 1950 and showing scenes form the life of Sant' Ambrogio, including his miraculous appearance at the battle of Parabiago in 1330. To the right of the central, Pogliaghi, doors is another set from 1950, the work of Franco Lombardi with scenes from the history of Milan. The fifth set was completed only in 1965 by Luciano Minguzzi with scenes from the building of the Duomo, and the life of San Carlo Borromeo.

Covering the façade are a fine array of statues which have survived the increasingly grim Milanese air remarkably well. The statuary is continued on the sides, where some of the better examples form a sub-section of the 96 giant gargoyles. From the façade and sides rise a mass of spires that form a small forest of stone through which to view Milan from the roof of the cathedral. There are both steps and lifts to the roof – two sets, one on each side of the apse – and a visit is a must. On very clear days (sadly, all too infrequent in Milan), the pre-Alps are visible to the north and the Apennines to the south. On such days the Lombardy Plain is also laid out in great detail. More usually, but no less spectacularly, the view is over the city and a visit to the roof offers a good opportunity to set the internal map and compass ready for walks of exploration.

A visit to the roof need not concern those afraid of heights or exposed positions: it is quite safe, with all drops well away from the visitor, and all exposed places neatly protected by wire mesh or clear plastic screens. The area is also wide and spacious, the main roof itself being quite remarkably formed with huge flat slabs of stone. Above it all rises the Madonnina, glinting in the sun. So attached are the Milanese to this symbol of their city that no building that is close to it is allowed to overtop it. (Indeed, it is only within the last thirty years or so that the skyscraper has arrived in Milan). The statue is much bigger than it looks; it is always foreshortened because of the need to look sharply upward, and is actually over 4 metres high.

While you are on the roof there is so much to look at that it is easy to miss some important feature. If you can go again this is no problem, but for the once-only visitor it is a great pity. So, be sure to pick out the campanile of San Gottardo, to the south beyond the Palazzo Reale, the Sforza castle, to the north-west, Corso Vittorio Emanuele II running away to the north-east, the Torre Velasca to the south and, if the weather is reasonable, the San Siro football stadium far away to the west.

Within the Duomo, if time allows and opportunity occurs, go to the remains of the paleo-Christian buildings that have been opened at the western (main door) end. The remains include a section of the first church, of St Tecla, but are chiefly of a baptistery built about the same time. The entrance to the site is close to the entrance doors. To the right of these doors is the stone commemorating the start of work, close to a superb copy – the original is in the Museum of the Duomo in Palazzo Reale; indeed, several of the statues and works of art in and on the Duomo are exact copies, with the originals being kept in the

Il Madonnina

67

A statue on the Duomo

museum – of a wood and copper eleventh-century crucifix marking the grave of an early Archbishop. Further along the right wall is a list of the Duomo Archbishops, a list that includes many men who went on to become Pope. This century there have been two, Pius XI and Paul VI.

Before the visitor has had the time to see the baptistery ruins, the plaques or the crucifix he will have spent time near the door. As eyes adapt to the darkness after the brightness of the Milanese day, the sheer size of the church that emerges from the gloom is enough to enthrall most visitors.

The red light that shines out from high up in the nave roofing indicates the position of a True Nail held in a glass reliquary at the centre of a crucifix. Tradition has the Nail being given to Sant' Ambrogio by the Emperor Constantine. During the Archbishopric of San Carlo Borromeo, a man we shall meet several times on our walks around Milan, the Nail was processed around the city at the height of an outbreak of plague, with immediate results. In November of each year the Nail is brought to the floor of the cathedral so it my be seen by the faithful. It is, somewhat surprisingly, shaped like a horse's bit. The procedure of bringing the nail down and taking it back up is performed using a small platform, worked by an ancient system of ropes and pulleys and known as *La Nivola*, the 'little cloud'.

Set into the floor near the entrance is a brass strip running the width of the building to a sundial set on the left wall. High in the roof a hole allows the sun to strike the brass line twice annually, on 21 June and 21 December, at noon. The Milanese used the event to reset watches and clocks at a time when there was no acceptable absolute measure of time. Sadly, however, subsidence of the building means that the sundial is no longer accurate.

Within the Duomo there is so much to see that a full inventory is impracticable. No one thing is outstanding, and in that way the cathedral compares somewhat unfavourably with other Milanese churches, the very specific treasures of, say, San Maurizio church do not detract from the sheer majesty of the cathedral. In any case, there *are* excellent works of sacred art in the Duomo. The right nave has several altars by Il Pellegrini, while at its end, in the right transept, is the tomb of Gian Giacomo Medici, known as *Il Medeghino*. As a young man Il

Medeghino was exiled from Milan to Lake Como for killing a man, and there he took over a castle on the natural fortress of the Sassoi di Musso near the village of Musso at the northern end of the lake, killing the castle's governor. From the castle he ruled the lake, more as pirate than governor, choosing just the right moment to sell the fortress to the Milanese during the time of the Spanish-French war. This remarkable *condottiere* – the word is pure Italian and does not translate at all well; it describes a mercenary, but perhaps 'soldier of fortune' is more polite and catches the flavour better – not only managed to hold on to his head, but to great booty as well. His brother, Pope Pius IV, had the tomb erected in 1564. It is decorative and interesting, with *Il Medeghino* shown between statues representing Peace and War. The tomb is the work of Leone Leoni whose own memorial, his house, stands close to the Duomo (see page 90).

Opposite the tomb, at the other side of the transept, is a statue of St Bartholomew, remarkable for its subject and for its conceit. The subject is the saint after his martyr's death, the result of being flayed alive, with his skin over his shoulder like a cloak; go around behind the statue to see the face, with hair, beard and eye holes. The anatomical detail of the muscles below the skin is alarming, but very much in keeping with the times, when there was a great interest in anatomical detail. The effect is macabre. The conceit comes from the inscription which, translated, reads 'Not Praxiteles but Marco d'Agrate carved me'. I fear that d'Agrate had an inflated opinion of his worth!

Around the corner is a work of Francesco Messina, a famous contemporary Italian sculptor whose studio is open to visitors. The work is of Pope Pius XI, the Milanese Archbishop Achille Ratti. The contrast between the two works is stark.

At the corner of the apse is a memorial tablet to the consecration of the Duomo by San Carlo Borromeo on 20 October 1577. In order to reach this tablet you will pass the entrance to the crypt that holds the Duomo treasury and the body of the saint himself.

San Carlo Borromeo was born in Arona on the western shore, but southern tip, of Lake Maggiore, in 1522. His birthplace was the town castle, a stronghold of the Borromeo family that held most of the western shoreline, as well as the castle of Angera on the opposite shore. Today their name is still associated with that latter castle, which the family owns, and also with the Borromean islands, Isola Bella and Isola Madre, that stand in the lake off Stresa. Carlo was made a cardinal at 22 and Archbishop of Milan at 26, though it has been suggested that these appointments were as much due to the boy's uncle being Pope Pius IV as to any inherent abilities. Nevertheless, during the time of his Archbishopric Carlo was a diligent worker for the Christian faith, a builder of churches and rooter-out of heretics. He was also a brave man, taking personal risks to comfort the sick during an outbreak of plague. Many years after his death Carlo was sanctified and a successor as Archbishop of Milan – another member of the Borromeo family, Federico – had a statue to him erected near Arona. It can be visited from Milan, and is worth the time. It is huge, over 23 metres tall, and can be climbed (on the inside). It shows San Carlo to have had a big nose and long ears, features which must have been real as they also appear in several portraits. To check, look at the portrait by Crepsi in the northern sacristy. But was he really too ugly, as some said, to be anything but a saint?

San Carlo's body lies in a silver and crystal casket given by Philip IV of Spain. The body is dressed in jewelled vestments, the face covered with a silver mask fashioned from a wax death mask. In comparison to the bodies in the crypt of the church of Sant' Ambrogio the burial is quite tasteful. On the way to the tomb there are some mementoes of the great man, a crucifix staff and a mitre.

Also in the crypt is the Duomo treasury, a pay-to-enter collection that is closed for a long period at lunch. The collection is small, but contains some delightful exhibits. Among these are silver reliquaries, a beautiful ivory cover (diptych) for an evangeliary, dating from the fifth-century and covered with early Christian designs and a later (early eleventh-century) cover for Archbishop Ariberto's evangeliary, a magnificent work in gold and enamel.

Back in the main body of the Duomo, after crossing the apse one of the building's great works will be found in the left (north) transept, the Trivulzio candelabrum. This, in finely-worked bronze inlaid with semi-precious stones, is thought to be by the twelfth-century French master Nicola de Verdun and was

70

Ariberto's Evangeliery, Duomo treasury

presented to the Duomo by Giovanni Battista Trivulzio in 1562. In Jewish tradition the candelabrum tree, which is five metres tall, has seven branches, and is inscribed with events from both the Old and New Testaments. In front of the tree is a group of tombs including that of Cardinal Federico Borromeo. The chapel of the transept, to the Madonna of the Tree, is by Francesco Maria Richini, an architect whose work adorns much of the city. The left (north) nave contains more altars by Il Pellegrini.

This short visit has ignored the stained glass of the Duomo, impressive for both its form and its size. Do look out for the windows.

Pallazzo Reale On the southern edge of Piazza del Duomo, beside the Duomo itself, a small irregular square opens out, the Piazzetta Reale. The *piazzetta* is formed by the Palazzo Reale, the royal palace (some pedants would say the *ex*-royal palace and its irregular shape is produced by the off-line main section of the building; the two 'arms' of the square are completed by two wings of the palace. These wings are (not surprisingly) of different lengths and knows as the *mancia corta* and the *mancia lunga* by the Milanese, the 'short sleeve' and the 'long sleeve'. Buildings on the site go back to the eleventh-century, when the town hall, the *Broletto Vecchio*, of the free city of Milan stood here. Later, under the Viscontis, the ducal palace occupied the site, although the dukes themselves moved into the castle following the murder of Giovanni Maria Visconti on the steps of the nearby church of San Gottardo. Following this move of the ducal seat the *palazzo* fell into disuse and disrepair, a state from which it only recovered when the Spanish governors took it over many years later. Later city rulers, the Austrians, tore down the original front wing of the building to turn a courtyarded palace into a three-winged palace around the *piazzetta*. The Austrians installed a theatre which was the scene of many of Mozart's early successes, including the performance of his first opera when he was all of fourteen years old. Unfortunately, in 1776 a fire burnt the theatre to the ground, and with the building of La Scala it was never rebuilt.

The statue of the Archangel Michael had its head removed in the seventeenth century by a marksman in the castle. The man fired a single bullet, and the decapitation of St Michael prevented him from suffering the same fate. He had been sentenced to death by the castle commander and had been given the chance to prove his prowess with a gun and so save his life.

After the numerous alterations the *palazzo* was renamed several times, becoming the Palazzo Nationale of the Cisalpine Republic and the Palazzo Reale, the royal palace, property of the Crown, following unification. Vittorio Emanuele III gave the *palazzo* to the city in 1920. During the allied bombings of 1943 it was very badly damaged and much of the internal work and stored archives were lost. Today the *palazzo*, an enormous Neo-classical building, the work of Piermarini whose workers toiled from 1770 and 1778 to transform the existing building on the site, houses the headquarters of several institutes of history and art.

The second floor also houses the museum of Contemporary Art. The exhibits cover an interesting range of work all the way from the frankly odd to the vaguely classical, but the gallery should be visited to gain an insight into the current position of Italian art. The colourful works of Tancredi are particularly appealing.

The Palazzo Reale also houses the Museum of the Duomo in which are held some of the original statues and other works from the cathedral. These include the original of the Crucifix of

Ariberto and the keystone cover for the apse, known as the *Padre Eterno*, the 'Eternal Father'. It is a fourteenth-century gilded copper work modelled on a design by Jacopino da Tradate. Several of the original spires of the cathedral are also here. The Hall of Columns has at its head a replica of the *raza*, wheel, of the Viscontis used as the central element of the largest of the apse windows. There is also a very fine wooden model of the Duomo, handy for a first look at the roof statuary before the visit.

A painting by Tancredi, Museum of Contemporary Art, Palazzo Reale

At the back of the Palazzo Reale, and reached from the Via Pecorari which runs behind it, is the church of San Gottardo. It was erected as a ducal chapel in 1336 by Azzone Visconti who was buried in it just three years later. In 1412 one of Azzone's descendants, Giovanni Maria Visconti, an unpleasant, unpopular man, was murdered on the steps of the church; with that, the ducal family moved into the castle. Once the church had a beautiful Gothic facade, but during renovation work on the Palazzo Reale in 1770 this was demolished to make way for a new main staircase. Today only the superb campanile and a section of the right side of the church remain from the original fourteenth-century building. By common consent this campanile is the finest in the city, and was built by the architect commemorated in the name of the street where the church entrance is found – Francesco Pecorari of Cremona. The campanile was the first in the city to have a clock that struck the hours (although that of the church of Sant' Eustorgio was the first to have had a clock, in 1306)

In its lower part the campanile is square, but it soon becomes octagonal, rising in elegant brickwork tiers separated by delicate friezes. The lower tiers have neat windows, but not one to each face of the octagon, while the upper tiers have windows in each face, beautiful windows with elegant marble columns. The campanile finishes with a galleried loggia, its conical roof topped with a gilded statue of the Archangel Michael.

On the inside, be sure to find the fresco of the crucifixion on the front wall. The fresco, completed in the fourteenth-century, was originally on an outside wall, near the campanile. At first it was attributed to an unknown painter of the Giotto school, but more recent academic opinion is hardening to the opinion that it is by the master himself. To the right of the High Altar there is also a fine canvas by Cerano showing St Charles.

73

Above
The Piermarini fountain and the Duomo

Right
The lantern above the entrance gate to the Palazzo Arcivescovile

Palazzo Arcivescovile To the east of Palazzo Reale, and still in the Piazza del Duomo, is the Palazzo Arcivescovile. The present *palazzo* was built in about 1170 on the site of an earlier episcopal seat destroyed by Barbarossa. After this initial rebuild, further work was carried out by several resident archbishops, most particularly San Carlo Borromeo who used his favourite architect Pelligrino Tibaldi (*Il Pellegrini*).

Externally the *palazzo* is severe and a little dull – though you should look for the symbol of the Viscontis, the snake eating the saracen – but inside it is exquisite, comprising two courtyards which are occasionally open to the visitor; as the *palazzo* now houses private offices, visiting is not unrestrained. The first, and larger courtyard, is the Archbishop's Court, but the smaller Canon's Court is the better. It is the work of *Il Pellegrini* and a masterpiece of clever stonework and simple, clean lines. The two statues on the walled side – there are three porticoed sides and one walled – are of San Carlo, the architect's boss and Sant' Ambrogio, the City's first bishop.

On the south side the *palazzo* has a strange addition, the Rotonda of Pellegrini. This was once known as San Carlo's Stable because of the archbishop's mules were kept on the ground floor, the horses of the higher clergy on the first floor and hay for the animals on the upper floor.

The eastern side of Palazzo Arcivescovile – with its entrance into Archbishop's Court – lies in the Piazza Fontana. The Piazza is named after the Piermarini fountain that stands at its centre. Milan has few fountains for so Mediterranean a city and this one, the oldest, was itself only built in 1782 to a design by Piermarini. It is very popular with the Milanese, and the seats around it are filled at most times of the day. From the square the view of the Duomo is tremendous and this, together with the surprising peace, due in large part to the absence of local traffic, makes Piazza Fontana a very pleasant spot to rest aching feet.

On the opposite side of the piazza from the Palazzo Arcivescovile is the Palazzo dei Tribunali, the imposing courts of justice, built in the late sixteenth-century and seeing service as both a jail and a courthouse. Today it houses the *Vigili Urbani*, one of the many factions of the Italian police forces.

La Rinascente Going around behind the apse of the Duomo the visitor passes the Palazzo dell'Orologio, named after the clock at the top, which is flanked by statues of night and day. The palazzo is also notable for the huge Corinthian columns that break up the façade.

Turning left back along the Duomo's side, you are between the outside of the northern transept and La Rinascente, a modern shopping area built in 1950 to replace one destroyed during World War II. The name is from the destroyed building, built in 1921 and called 'The Re-born' by Gabriele D'Annuzio, hero or villain – depending on your interpretation – of the Fiume expedition. Tacked on to the back of the building is the church of San Raffaele, entered from Via San Raffaele. This is an early church, dating from the ninth-century, which was rebuilt under the direction of San Carlo Borromeo. Inside there are three naves, as there were in the original church, and several fine paintings. In the chapel on the right of the entrance is a painting

Galleria Vittorio Emanuele

depicting St Matthew and the Angel, the work of Ambrogio Figino, an artist who died in 1608, while in the presbytery there is a fine canvas by Cerano (Giovan Battista Crespi). The choir contains some interesting Flemish frescoes.

Galleria Vittorio Emanuele Further along is the justifiably famed Galleria Vittorio Emanuele which links the cathedral square with that of La Scala. It is the most beautiful covered walkway in Italy and also the first in which metal and glass were used as structural elements rather than purely for adornment.

The gallery was begun in 1865, soon after the unification of northern Italy, and took thirteen years to complete. The last element to be added was the magnificent triumphal arch at the entrance from the Piazza del Duomo. This takes a similar form to the Arch of Peace and is set off by the extended, arcaded arms that drift along the edge of the square. The Gallery is formed like a Latin cross, 196 metres along the longer arm, 105 metres along the shorter, the central section being octagonal. This central part, with its huge and impressive glass cupola, was once decorated with niched statues, but these have been removed as they were too difficult to keep clean. Now only the four mosaics

76

Above
The roof of the Galleria

Left
Savini, the Galleria's most famous restaurant

representing Europe, Asia, Africa and America together with those representing Agriculture, Art, Science and Industry remain. At the La Scala end the architect was faced with a difficulty of geometry, the Piazza delle Scala being offset from the Piazza del Duomo. If the line of the Gallery was maintained then the exit to La Scala would have been equally off line. To get over this problem the latter exit is gently angled so that from La Scala the exit/entrance is square to the Piazza. So good is this solution that many visitors only recognise the change of angle when viewing the Gallery from the top of the Duomo.

The Gallery is known as *Il salotto di Milano*, the 'drawing room of Milan', being the traditional meeting place of the Milanese, who use it at all times of day attracted by the city's best cafés and restaurants, together with a range of fine shops whose windows are dressed by masters in the craft. Among the restaurants is the Savini, Milan's most prestigious, where opera–goers congregate after a performance to while away the rest of the evening in expensive surroundings. As a contrast, the Gallery has the Magic Restaurant, the best sandwich bar which also sells pizza and coffee, ice cream and soft drinks. The Galleria is also the location of a SIP office for those wanting to make telephone calls.

Piazza della Duomo from the roof of the Duomo

West of the Duomo Westward of the Duomo across the Piazza del Duomo, one of the finest sweeps of paved pedestrian walkway in Europe and, thankfully, not badly scarred by the two entrances to the new Metro Line 3, is a monument to Vittorio Emanuele II, a bronze equestrian statue by Ercole Rosa dating from 1896. The king is shown as he appeared at the battle of San Martino, the basal frieze showing the entry into Milan of Piedmontian and French troops following the battle of Magenta.

The extreme western edge of the square has the now compulsory big city billboards extolling the virtues of consumerism. It is in keeping with the teams of hawkers and stallholders in the square offering flapping birds, ice creams and drinks, postcards, souvenirs and packets of seed for the apparently endless flock of pigeons. It is also in keeping with the history of the square which has always been the centre for vendors and street artists. In ancient times one regular performer apparently used to swallow stones and then make music by banging on his stomach.

Piazza dei Mercanti Via Mercanti leads off from the north-west corner of the square. Very soon this leads to an arcaded building on the left, the arcades forming a raised dais that is usually home to another flock of pigeons. Go left here into Piazza Mercanti.

Although close to the Piazza del Duomo and its hubbub of city life, and surrounded by cars, the Piazza Mercanti manages to preserve a little of the quiet that must occasionally have existed in Medieval, pre-car, times. Some have bemoaned the fast food outlet that has now taken over the odd corner of the Piazza, but this is the site of the ancient Milanese *fiera* (fair) – the name itself means Square of the Merchants – and doubtless on fair days the Piazza was not the ocean of calm many claim it must have been.

In Medieval times all the city's most important public buildings were here, standing in a closed square linked with the rest of the city and reached only through one of six gates or vaults, each of which corresponded to a gate in the old city wall. The most important building was the Broletto or Palazzo della Ragione, the Righteous House, so called because the judges for both civil and penal cases sat there. On the west side of the piazza were the offices of the city governor and the prison; to the east was the college of lawyers; to the north were the offices of the public magistrates; to the south, at the Portico della Ferrata, public auctions were held. The piazza itself was filled with the stalls of local merchants and shopkeepers.

At the centre of the square is a well which, until 1879, was the other side of the Palazzo della Ragione. At that time the square was bigger, with the palazzo standing at its centre, and the northern limit being the Palazzo Giureconsulti which now stands on the far side of Via Mercanti. The well was moved because of this road, which went through its original position, although it was not put into its present position until 1921. It was originally a public well, but fell into disuse in the late sixteenth-century.

The Palazzo della Ragione, also known as the Broletto Nuovo, is the oldest and most important surviving example of Romanesque Milanese civic architecture. *Broletto* is the 'little' version of *brolo* which in the Middle Ages was a tree-lined meadow, a place where, traditionally, the Archbishop dispensed justice. In the newly emerging cities this meadow was symbolized

79

Serpent wall ring, Piazza dei Mercanti

in the Broletto, even after the communes had taken all powers in the making of laws and handing out of justice away from the church. In time the cities chose to further stamp their authority on the matter by calling these new palaces of justice the Palazzo della Ragione rather than the Broletto. In many cities the names are still interchangeable, a fact that has given many a visitor a mystified look.

The 'new' building was erected in 1229 to replace the Broletto Vecchio, the old Broletto, which stood near the present Piazzetta Reale. The building was sanctioned by Oldrado da Tresseno in his capacity as the city governor, and the city's chief magistrate sat in the huge room on the first floor flanked by two judges who adjudicated for the civil and criminal trials. These two judges were called the horse and the hen, because it was said, they needed to have the swiftness of the one and the vigilance of the other. Later, the Palazzo played host to the *Consiglio dei Novacento*, the Counsel of the 900, 150 counsellors from each of the six 'gate' districts of the city. Francis I of France reduced the number to 60, and a later Austrian ruler abolished the counsel altogether. In 1786 the city's administrative offices were transferred to the Palazzo del Carmagnola – which instantly became know as the Broletto Nuovissino, the *very* new Broletto!

Externally the Palazzo della Ragione is a column–arcade-supported rectangular brick building, elegant and business-like, as one might expect. The relief on the square side is of Governor Tresseno and is attributed to Benedetto Antelami. Under the statue is an inscription mentioning Tresseno – *Dominum Oldradus de Trexeno, Pot (estas) Mediolani* – and dated MCCXXXIII, 1233, making it the oldest equestrian statue in Milan.

Look, too for the iron horse rings on the wall below the relief, each of the rings held by a Visconti snake. On the Via Mercanti side of the *palazzo* is a relief sculpture of the 'half wool sow', the mythical half-pig, half-sheep that legend had it was the real derivation of the name Mediolanum – from *medio lanae*. That theory has now been replaced in the minds of all but the most incurable romantics by the idea that the name derives from *medio e lanus*, half-way plain, *lanus* being a Celtic corruption of *plane*.

Access to the *palazzo*, basically one huge room measuring 50 metres by 18 metres, is by a stone bridge.

Across from the Palazzo della Ragione the most impressive building is the Palazzo delle Scoule Palatine, the Pallatine School, built in 1645 by the architect Carlo Buzzi as a copy of the Palazzo dei Giureconsulti – proving perhaps that imitation is indeed the sincerest form of flattery. It occupies the site of a former school that was razed by fire. The Pallatine School was reserved for the teaching of the law, rhetoric, medicine and mathematics. In niches above the arcade are statues of St Augustine, to the left, and the fourth-century poet Ausino, who dedicated some of his most famous verses to the city. These verses are on the tablet to the left, the right tablet being a celebration of the Spanish governor Pietro Giorgio Burro who was responsible for the school's construction.

To the left of the Pallatine School – looking from the well – is the Loggia degli Osii, an elegant fourteenth-century building of black and white marble built by Matteo Visconti. Major alterations in the seventeenth and eighteenth-centuries covered

Palazzo della Ragione, Piazza dei Mercanti

Palazzo della Ragione, Piazza dei Mercanti

up the marble and we have to be grateful to renovations in 1904 for the fact that it is now visible again. The statue of the Virgin at the centre of the building is a work of the Maestro Campionesi, a group of sculptors and architects working out of what is now an enclave of Italy entrenched in Switzerland, Campione d'Italia. This group is remarkable not only for the quality of its work, but also for the fact that no individual has ever been known by name; only the corporate identity has come down across the years. The balcony in the centre of the building shows the Visconti snake emblem together with the Imperial eagle and the mythical half-sheep, half-pig. From this balcony, the city *palera*, or public proclamations were made.

Forming the other part of the arched passage of the Pallatine School is the Palazzo dei Notai, the lawyer's house, sometimes known as the Palazzo dei Panigarola, which held the city Statute Office where the acts and orders of the city governors were held. It is a fine building, an example of fifteenth-century Gothic, with a good sculpted figure of Hercules as a child under the last on the right of the four arches. Underneath one of the porticos is a memorial plaque that bemoans the fact that in any dispute it is only ever the lawyers who grow fat!

Today the *palazzo* houses, in its lower left side, the restaurant of the Piazza dei Mercanti. To sit here, or much better, outside under the sun umbrellas, is one of the great pleasures of a visit to Milan. The city traffic is distant enough to be a world away, so your meal will be served in almost perfect surroundings and will also be peaceful.

The Palazzo dei Giureconsulti, which formed the old northern edge of the Piazza dei Mercanti, was built in the sixteenth-century by order of the Milanese Pope Pius IV as a college for jurists. Here the children of the rich and famous, children destined to take over the city's highest offices, were trained. Although it was begun in the sixteenth-century the building was not actually completed for over a hundred years, the upper floor being added in the seventeenth-century. When the college closed in 1797 the building housed several city departments, and now houses the chamber of commerce.

The outside of the building is decorated in fine style, but the eye is drawn to the centre of the façade, to the ancient tower of the city commune, built in 1272 but later remodelled in Baroque style. The clock at half height was added in 1601. In a niche at the base is a statue of Sant' Ambrogio which, in 1833, replaced one of Philip II of Spain. Before the complete replacement the head had been removed from Philip's statue in 1797 and replaced by one showing the tyrant Brutus.

Inside, the *palazzo* was originally decorated with numerous fine frescoes, but many of these did not survive the war years. Of those that did, the best is on the vaulted ceiling of what was a college chapel but is now a space occupied by a marble staircase, This is a Glory of Angels and was painted by the Neapolitan artist Giovan Battista Sassi who worked in the city during the early years of the eighteenth-century.

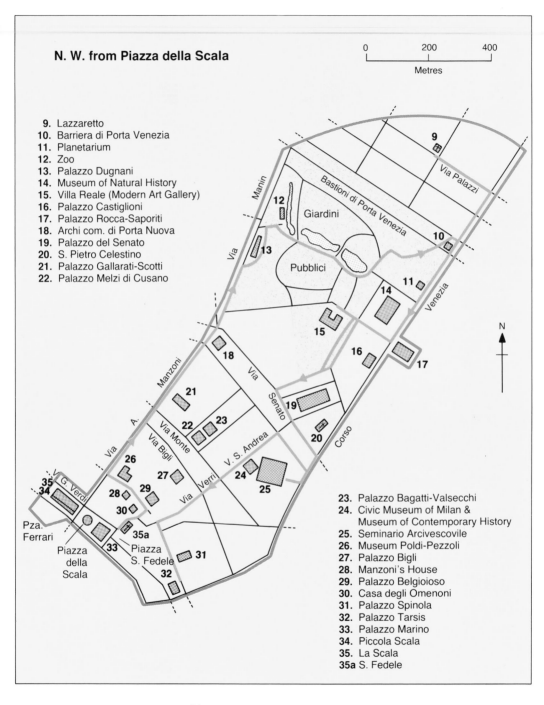

N. W. from Piazza della Scala

0   200   400

Metres

9. Lazzaretto
10. Barriera di Porta Venezia
11. Planetarium
12. Zoo
13. Palazzo Dugnani
14. Museum of Natural History
15. Villa Reale (Modern Art Gallery)
16. Palazzo Castiglioni
17. Palazzo Rocca-Saporiti
18. Archi com. di Porta Nuova
19. Palazzo del Senato
20. S. Pietro Celestino
21. Palazzo Gallarati-Scotti
22. Palazzo Melzi di Cusano

23. Palazzo Bagatti-Valsecchi
24. Civic Museum of Milan &
    Museum of Contemporary History
25. Seminario Arcivescovile
26. Museum Poldi-Pezzoli
27. Palazzo Bigli
28. Manzoni's House
29. Palazzo Belgioioso
30. Casa degli Omenoni
31. Palazzo Spinola
32. Palazzo Tarsis
33. Palazzo Marino
34. Piccola Scala
35. La Scala
35a S. Fedele

North-west from Piazza della Scala

Palazzo Marino At the far end of the Galleria Vittorio Emanuele from the Piazza del Duomo is Piazza della Scala, the second most famous of the Milanese squares. Although it is the theatre of La Scala that visitors come to see, the Palazzo Marino, to the right of the Galleria exit, dominates the square.

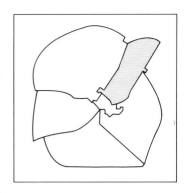

For many years this *palazzo* has been considered the most beautiful private house in Milan. Indeed, the man for whom the *palazzo* was built claimed it was the most beautiful house in Christendom.

The *palazzo* was started in 1558 by Galeazzo Alessi, another very famous Milanese architect, for a rich merchant, Tomaso Marino, its starting date explaining the delightful blend of Renaissance and Baroque styles. The size of the *palazzo*, and the intricacy of its design ensured a very long building period, the main staircase being completed only at the end of the century, after Alessi's death. The work continued under another architect, but the death of Marino, combined with the vast expense of the building together with the losses his surviving family also suffered at the hands of the new Spanish governors, meant that work stopped altogether for many years. Ultimately the Marino family surrendered the site to the governor who sold it on to another Milanese businessman, Carlo Omodeo, who did at least allow a member of the Marino family to live in part of it – at an agreed rent. Finally, in the second half of the eighteenth-century the *palazzo* returned to the city and used as an extension of the town hall. The building was eventually completed in 1880, over 300 years after the first stone had been laid. By contrast, when the *palazzo* was badly damaged in World War II, the rebuilding took a mere nine years.

When contemplating the history of the *palazzo* you have to wonder whether there might not have been some truth in an ancient prophecy made at the time when Alessi began work on the building. It was stated in Latin – although by whom and to whom no one is sure – and the original read *Aut uret, aut ruet, aut alter raptor rapiet* which translates as, 'either it will burn, or it will fall down or another thief will take possession of it.' I was told by a Milanese, with a wry smile, that it was as well the prophet had not heard of smog, or that would have been included as well.

Externally the *palazzo* is genuinely four-sided, I say 'genuinely' because although all buildings are four-sided (unless they are triangular), each of the four sides cannot always be viewed and walked along as they can here. The better, three-tiered sides face the Piazza della Scala and the Piazza San Fedele. Each tier is pierced by a symmetrical row of windows, the windows varying very slightly from floor to floor – double with rectangle and square, as before but with arched, decorated lintel, single with triangular lintel – and the whole is finished with a stone balustrade.

Inside there are two fine courtyards, the larger, the *Cortile d'Onore*, is quite beautiful with a double loggia supported by double columns. In Italy the *palazzo* has a literary claim to fame because in one of the rooms overlooking Piazza San Fedele Virginia Marino, wife of the son of the first Spanish governor of Milan, gave birth to a daughter, Marianna, who became the 'Nun of Monza' celebrated in a well-known Italian novel.

Leonardo Monument The Piazza della Scala was created in 1859-60 when several old buildings between what is now La Scala and the Palazzo Marino were pulled down. The last buildings to be completed were those of the Banca Commerciale which were only finished in the first quarter of the twentieth-century. At the centre of the square is a monument to Leonardo da Vinci by Pietro Magni, completed in 1872. The monument comprises a statue of the great man on a plinth of red granite, the plinth protected by four of Leonardo's favourite pupils, Marco d'Oggiono, Cesare da Sesto, Andrea Solaino and Giovanni Antonio Boltraffio. The decoration on the monument is intended to convey the idea of Leonardo as artist, sculptor, architect and engineer.

La Scala Beyond the Leonardo monument and the row of yellow taxis, each with a driver whose disregard for your safety if you try to cross the road in front of them is as remarkable as any of da Vinci's theories, is La Scala. The theatre of La Scala was completed by 1778 by Giuseppe Piermarini following the decision by City Governor Ferdinand Hapsburg not to rebuild the theatre in the Palazzo Reale which had just burned down for the third time. The site for the new theatre was given by the governor, but the money for its building was donated by the Milanese, mostly the rich who bought boxes well in advance. The theatre was completed in the very short time of two years.

Stendhal, on his return to his adopted city after an absence of two years, claimed La Scala to be the most important opera in the world, since which time no one has felt the need, or had the temerity, to fault his judgement. The theatre was built on the site of the old church of Santa Maria della Scala which had been founded in 1381 by Beatrice della Scala, wife of Bernabo Visconti. Those visitors who know Verona will recognize the name della Scala, since both the city and its neighbourhood – particularly the eastern shore of Lake Garda – are well endowed with castles of the family, also frequently known as the Scaligeri. The family took as their emblem a ladder, hence the family name, hence the name of the church and hence the name of the opera house. Piermarini's new theatre was inaugurated on 3 August 1778 with the work *L'Europe Riconsciuta* by Antonio Salieri

In its earliest days – when the theatre was used for balls and as a gaming house of, at one time, ill repute – the theatre was decorated in Baroque style, but in 1807 it was redecorated in Neo-Classical style only to be redecorated yet again in 1830 by

Piazza della Scala, with the Leonardo monument and La Scala

87

Antonio Sanquirico. The theatre was very badly damaged by the bombings of 1943 and the first of the city's monuments to be rebuilt, when the original was faithfully recreated. On the evening of 11 May 1946 La Scala was officially reopened with a performance of *La Gazza Ladra*, conducted by Arturo Toscanini who travelled from the United States specially.

Externally La Scala is straightforwardly Neo-Classical with absolutely no pretentions. Indeed, the visitor could be forgiven for being a little disappointed, although when it is floodlit at night the theatre very much comes to life. Inside there are busts of the great composers – Bellini, Donizetti, Rossini and Verdi – and one of Stendhal, presumably in thanks for his kind words. The auditorium is horseshoe-shaped with four tiers of boxes and two galleries and is very luxuriously decorated with friezes and gilded stuccoes in Neo-Classical style. The lighting is aided by the famed Lampadrio di Boemia chandelier installed in 1923 which has 365 light bulbs, one for every day of the year. The stage covers nearly 800 square metres, the largest in Europe, and its size is further enhanced by the optical trick of its being slightly sloped. In theory the theatre can hold about 2,800 people, although new security measures limit this on most occasions to around 2,000.

La Scala's season starts – in very grand style – on Sant' Ambrogio's Day, 7 December, and continues until the end of May. There are concerts during June and from September until November, with a short ballet season in September.

Those who do no have the time to go to a La Scala performance or are visiting out of season, must make do with going to the theatre museum; this normally, but not always, includes a trip to the auditorium. The theatre museum was opened in 1913 and holds many important records and documents, as well as busts and drawings of musicians and famous singers who have performed at La Scala, together with more general information on the history of the theatre. The collection of Verdi memorabilia is particularly impressive, with several manuscripts in his own hand. There is also a fine library on the history of opera, a collection of eighteenth and nineteenth-century musical instruments, posters from early works in the theatre and masks and statues for Roman and Greek theatre.

To the left of La Scala is Via Filodrammatici. At No.2 is the Piccola Scala, the 'little Scala', a small theatre that is part of the La Scala complex and in which are performed modern, experimental works, rare operas and concerts of chamber music. The theatre also offers the chance for singers and players who are starting out on their careers to make a first impression. Occasionally plays are also performed. The first work was *Matrimonio Segreto* (Secret Marriage) by Cimarosa on the night of 26 December 1955. The Little Scala holds about 600 people. Also in Via Filodrammatici, at No.1, is a door that is worth a quick look. The portal of Palazzo Vimercati is no ordinary door, but the rarest and one of the most elegant Gothic Renaissance doors for many a mile. The door, – like most of the building that originally stood around it! – is mid-fifteenth-century and through it went members of the family whose name is now attached to it, even though the family *palazzo* was elsewhere. When that *palazzo* fell into disrepair the door was brought here, to Via Filodrammatici, where it was set up at the entrance to a convent. Look especially for the sculpted form of Francesco Sforza, modestly flanked by Julius Ceasar and Alexander the Great, and for the nail heads, a unique Milanese example.

Piazza San Fedele On the far side of Palazzo Marino from Piazza della Scala is the church of San Fedel, an interesting building. It is of Romanesque – and apparently unfinished – brickwork at its Via Catena end, and of the most beautifully finished Baroque style on the façade that overlooks Piazza San Fedele. In fact, this is probably the most completely original church from the sixteenth-century in Milan and has a long history of being attended by the rich and powerful. Another church built at the wish of San Carlo Borromeo, it was started in 1569 and, when completed, 'given' to the Jesuits who still look after it today. Since the church was the work of Pelligrini Tibaldi it means that at one time the two most famous of Milanese architects – *Il pellegrino* and *L'Alessi* – were working in Piazza San Fedele at the same time, the one on the church, and the other on the Palazzo Marino.

The church doorway is splendid, flanked by columns and elegantly arched, a neat balcony above it, set in an elaborate second tier, the whole under a triangular gable section. Many have seen more than a hint of Greek architecture about the Baroque façade.

The church of San Fedele and the Manzoni statue

In the Piazza outside the church of San Fedele is a monument by Alessandro Manzoni who was a regular worshipper at San Fedele. The monument, by Barzaghi, was completed when the writer was old and in poor health, as can be seen. It is sad that he could not have been turned so as to face his favourite church. Perhaps the decision was made because it was here that Manzoni fell when attempting to negotiate a stairway with more enthusiasm than regard for his age. Although he survived the blow to his head, the accident turned out to be the start of a rapid decline and he died just a few months later.

Inside there are several excellent canvasses worth your time, but it is the wood carving that holds the attention. The sacristy, reached after the second altar on the right, is widely believed to be the most beautiful in Milan because of the carved cupboards, the work of Giovanni Taurino, a master carver who was also responsible for the confessionals which he completed in 1596. Look too for the frescoed Madonna in the chapel of the Madonna dei Torriani, once known as the Madonna di Ballarin, the Madonna of the Ballerinas, because it was beloved of the dancers of La Scala. They would come to San Fedele on the morning after a show with bunches of flowers to offer as gifts to the Madonna in gratitude for their safety during the performance.

From the Piazza San Fedele it is a short step to see the brickwork of the church's north-eastern end, and to view the Casa degli Omenoni, the House of the Giants. The house was built in 1573 by the sculptor Leone Leoni, (an example of whose work we have seen in the Duomo). Leoni had it built for his private use and pleasure, decorating it with eight giant caryatids who stand guard on either side of the door. The caryatids were sculpted not by Leoni himself, but by Antonio Abbondio working to drawings by the owner. On the columns are the names of peoples defeated by Rome. Above them the lavish sculpture

continues with a graphic depiction of a man being eaten by lions, a play on Leoni's name. (The part of the man being bitten by the lion on the left is enough to bring the tears to anyone's eyes; I wonder if the sculptor would have liked to have done that to someone he knew). Leoni was an adventurer in the service of Charles V and Phillip II of Spain, and also claimed – rightly, it would appear – to have seen service at the oar of a rowed galley.

Piazza Belgioioso Go past the House of Giants, along Via Omenoni, named after the big men, and you will reach, to the left, the Piazza Belgioioso, another delightful and very fine quiet square. To the right is the Palazzo Belgioioso d'Este, dominating the square's north-eastern side, the *palazzo* of the family whose name – which appears to have just too many vowels – the square takes. It is a huge and ostentatiously rich house built around 1780 by Piermarini for Prince Antonio Barbiano di Belgioioso and his son, Albercio, who married Princess Anna Ricciarda d'Este. (Her family home, now the Hotel Villa d'Este, has astounded many visitors to Cernobbio on the western shore of Lake Como.) The Prince and his son wanted, it is said, a *palazzo* worthy of their station in life. It seems that they got their way. The pair's desire for recognition even extended to having the family name carved in the paving slabs of the piazza outside the *palazzo* and one or two of these can still be seen.

Left
Piazza Belgioioso with the Palazzo to the right and Casa Manzoni at the far end

Above
A 'giant' on Casa degli Omenoni

91

Ahead of you as you walk along the length of the piazza is the Casa del Manzoni, Manzoni's house, a fine nineteenth-century building in which the writer lived from 1813 until his death on 22 May 1873. It now houses the National Centre of Manzonian studies, with a precious and extensive library, consulting and reading rooms and the Manzoni Museum which includes one wing of the house left exactly as it was when the writer was alive. Two things are immediately impressive in this part of the wing: firstly, the austere nature of the furniture. Manzoni was a modest man and never enjoyed the standards of living which his fame would have allowed – the bedroom has a simple iron bed, the fireplace is small, the armchairs ordinary. I wonder how Manzoni must have felt as he gazed out of his window at the Palazzo Belgioioso and the comings and goings of Prince Albercio; the Prince rode out of the square each day on a horse, dressed in a bright general's uniform, in order to review the private bodyguard he equipped and maintained.

The second impression is less tangible – the curious feeling you get when you realize that those books on the shelves are Manzoni's books, the ones he read or consulted. The sense of the writer's presence in the museum is very real.

Antonio Pollaiolo's *Profile of a Young Woman*, Poldi-Pezzoli Museum

You can also visit the room of Tommaso Grossi, Manzoni's lawyer friend who practised from the house. Elsewhere, be sure to see the full-size portrait of the writer (known as *Il Grande* by the Italians) by de Notaris, completed after Manzoni's death, the exact dimensions of the man having been collected by post-mortem measuring. There is also an impressive collection of first editions.

Of Manzoni's work only *Il Promessi Sposi* – translated into English as *The Betrothed* – is well known to the English-speaking world. Manzoni was born, in 1785, near Lake Como and *The Betrothed* is set near Lecco on the eastern arm of that lake. The book was praised by Goethe and by Sir Walter Scott, who called it the finest book ever written. It is now accepted as his masterpiece and has spawned a small industry in northern Italy. Near Lake Como there is even an annual cycle race that visits the sites mentioned in the book.

Poldi-Pezzoli Museum From the Casa Manzoni it is a short step only to the street that carries the writer's name. Go right here to reach almost immediately the Poldi-Pezzoli Museum and one of the most prestigious private art collections in the world. The museum began as a purely private collection by Gian Giacomo Poldi-Pezzoli in the last half of the nineteenth-century and was given by him to the city when he died in 1879. The collector was born in Milan in 1822, inheriting great wealth from his father Giuseppe Poldi-Pezzoli who had inherited Parma estates from his Poldi father and wealth from his mother's family, the Pezzoli of Bergamo. In addition, Gian Giacomo inherited an accepted position in Milanese society from his mother Rosa Trivulzio, a member of a family whose superb chapel you can see in the basilica of San Nazaro. The young Gian did not take up his position in society, however, preferring to travel and to spend his money on his collection. Although seriously damaged in World War II the museum has now been returned to its original magnificence.

Room of Clocks, Poldi-Pezzoli Museum

The museum is housed in a seventeenth-century *palazzo*, although only the Baroque façade is original, the interior having been completely remodelled in the eighteenth-century. Today that interior decoration forms part of the museum itself, rather than acting merely as a backdrop to the works of art on display. The museum extends to about twenty rooms on two floors, and the visit starts with a room of ancient weaponry and then moves on to rooms that contain sacred parchments and vestments – some with designs from the school of Leonardo – and lace.

The staircase to the upper floor is in beautiful style, with a fountain at its base and leads to the more important art treasures. The first room contains fine works by Lombard artists, including Bernardino Luini, Zenale and Boltraffio. There is a room of ceramics, including pieces from the Miessen, Doccia and Capodimonte factories, and then the Black Room, so called because its walls were originally covered with ebony inlaid with ivory. Here there are some fine early sacred paintings. In the Dante Room that leads off the Bedroom (which contains a collection of early Murano glass) is a magnificent stained-glass windows by Giuseppe Bertini, dating from the mid-nineteenth-century. Two rooms of paintings, including further work by Boltraffio as well as superb panels by Tiepolo, are divided by a room of jewellery which includes some Renaissance bronzework.

The best-known work in the Poldi-Pezzoli is to be found in the Golden Room. This room has a Deposition by Sandro

Botticelli, works by Piero della Francesca and Andrea Mantegna and the museums's most famous work, the *Profile of a Young Lady* by Antonio Pollaiolo, now used as a symbol of the Poldi-Pezzoli and a painting that adorns the face of many Milanese tourist brochures – including one on the city's museums in which it has been reproduced the wrong way round!

Beyond the Golden Room is a further room of art and then a temperature-controlled room of old clocks, one of the finest collections in Italy. The clocks date from the sixteenth-century through to the nineteenth-century.

North along Via Manzoni Continuing northwards along the Via Manzoni the visitor reaches, to the right, Via Bigli, named after the Palazzo Bigli about 120 metres down the street on the right-hand side. The *palazzo* is an excellent town house dating from the early sixteenth-century, although almost all that you see now is from a remodelling in 1841. It is worth seeing for its two marble medallions which show the Annunciation, with the angel on the left and the Virgin Mary on the right, the work of Agostino Busti. Busti, who completed the reliefs in the early sixteenth-century, was known as *Il Bambaia*, another to have acquired a curiously Milanese nickname. The other noticeable thing about the *palazzo* is the motto: *Alta quid miraris tecta. Intus nil nisi benignum et humile.* This translates as 'Why are you marvelling at this exceptional house. Inside reigns only courtesy and modesty.'

The next road to the right, Via Montenapoleone, is by common consent the finest shopping street in Milan, the main thoroughfare of an area of 'high class' shopping. For details of the street's potential for the window (and real) shopper, see pages 27–30; here are all the great names of Italian shopping including Gucci, Missoni, Armani, Krizia, and jewellery shops of Beccellati and Calderoni, as well as leather shops and shoe shops.

In this famous road is Palazzo Melzi di Cusano, once one of the most important centres for Milanese high life. The *palazzo* dates from the mid-nineteenth-century and was built for Count Melzi di Cusano. It suits the Via Montenapoleone perfectly, with a wonderful elegance that is accentuated by the pastel colour of the façade, and the portico in the form of an Ionic temple with four huge columns.

Via Montenapoleone

The Palazzo Melzi di Cusano is at the corner of the Via San Spirito in which stands the Palazzo Bagatti-Valsecchi, soon to be another of Milan's fine series of museums. This *palazzo* is actually two buildings, one on each side of the road, built by brothers in the late nineteenth-century. No. 7 is in fifteenth-century Lombardy style, while No. 10 is in sixteenth-century Neo-Renaissance style. Between the two is the road, and a small piazzetta that takes the *palazzo's* name. The combination was built to accommodate the brothers' collection of Lombardy *objets d'art*, and these – ivories, terracotta, furniture, sculptures, bronzes and ceramics – will form a new museum when the necessary building work is completed. This museum (eastern) *palazzo* is elegant, its inner courtyard façade topped by a fine clock. In the courtyard is the Madonna of the Mouse, so called because of the mouse sitting on the shoulder of the baby. The opposite *palazzo* is private, but the view to the small arcaded courtyard, especially if it is sunlit, is enough to make you yearn to have spent time in Renaissance Milan.

Back in Via Manzoni, continue north to pass the church of San Francesco di Paola, a fine example of what might be termed flowery Baroque. At the top of the façade is the motto of the order of the

Little Fathers of San Francesco di Paolo who built the church: *Charitas*, charity. Inside is a huge fresco, the Glory of San Francesco di Paola, some fine wood carving and a High Altar in marble. Beside the church is Palazzo Gallarati-Scotti, a sixteenth-century building, substantially remodelled in the eighteenth-century. Behind the clean and tidy façade – I especially like the shutters, especially those of the top row of windows – is a fine cobbled courtyard.

North again, Via Manzoni ends at the *Arches Communale* of Porta Nuova, the most beautiful of the three ancient doors in the town walls. Originally the gate was in wood, but after the destruction of the city by Barbarossa it was rebuilt, in 1171, in brick. The gate is probably indicative of the way the new wall looked when it was eventually completed by Azzone Visconti in the thirteenth-century. Some of the sculptures and stones now in the gate were taken from the *Porta Orientale* (the eastern gate) which was demolished in 1819. On the outer, country, side of the gate the stonework is a pleasant mix of pale Roman marble and brown Lombard stones.

Through the arches is Piazza Cavour, named after the hero of the Risorgimento, a piazza that gives on to the Giardini Pubblici (Public Gardens), one of several splendid oases of green in the city. Before crossing the gardens go first along the western edge, up Via Manin, to reach the Palazzo Dugnani. The *palazzo* was built in the early seventeenth-century and after spending a period as one of the centres of Milanese high life it was taken over by a prestigious academy, the Accademia dei Fenici. Later it passed to the city and was the first site for the Natural History Museum. Externally it is very grand, its grandness enhanced by the off-setting of its constituent blocks.

Inside the *palazzo* is the Museum of Cinema and Italian Cinematography. Although the title suggests a wider scope, the museum is in fact wholly Italian and consists of photographs and posters, a marvellous collection of early cameras and sound-recording equipment. There is an extensive library too. Also within the *palazzo* is the *Spazio Baj*, a permanent exhibition of the ultra-modern engravings and collages of the artist Enrico Baj.

Giardini Pubblici The public gardens beside the *palazzo* were laid out in 1784 by Giuseppe Piermarini who started by uniting the gardens and orchards of several monasteries. The gardens were later enlarged by annexing a few more gardens so

**Left
Miniature train, Public
Gardens**

**Below
The Barriera di Porta Venezia**

that the total area is now nearly 18 hectares (about 44 acres). Most of the area is a garden in English style, with a remarkable number of native Italian trees and shrubs, together with some exotics. Within the garden boundaries are not only the Natural History Museum, the Planetarium, the City Zoo and the Palazzo Dugnani, but also the small hill of Monte Merlo, several springs, a lake and ten monuments to important Milanese inhabitants of the nineteenth-century (the Top Ten, as it were.) Here too is a tiny guage railway which offers children one or more trips around a small circuit that includes a tunnel. Elsewhere there are fine leafy walks and excellent play areas. The zoo, on a small site, has a varied collection chiefly of Italian animals but including some foreign species. It will soon be moved to another site where, it is hoped, the animals will have more natural surroundings.

The eastern edge of the gardens is defined by Corso Venezia, a road that ends at the Barriera di Porta Venezia. This is an interesting monument because the architect, Rodolfo Vantini, who completed the work in 1828, wanted to get away from the conventional Roman triumphal arch, (a decision said to have been as much due to the local inhabitants complaining that they did not want their view of the Lombardian Pre-Alps blocked as to any creative urge). The structure is two identical cuboids, each with a smaller cube on top, added later to confer greater importance to the monument. Note the little half-moon windows and the niches with their statues of pagan gods. The bas-reliefs show scenes from the history of Milan.

Around Porta Venezia Northward from Porta Venezia is a site with little enough to show the visitor but an impressive place in the Medieval history of both Milan and Europe. During the two-hundred-year period from the mid-fifteenth to the mid-seventeenth-centuries plague swept Europe, different countries reacting in different ways. In Milan the victims and suspected victims – and it is hard to believe that non-sufferers ever survived being suspected sufferers – were herded in to a custom-built enclosure. Based on the combination of the name of a similar building in Venice, Santa Maria di Nazareth, and the patron saint of plague victims, San Lazzaro, the Milan building was called the Lazzaretto. The building was huge, almost 14 hectares (about 35 acres) according to contemporary records, and was elegantly porticoed by *Il Filarete*. There was even a church for the victims, dedicated to San Carlo Borromeo who had an earlier one replaced. It is doubtful whether the unfortunates impounded in the Lazzaretto had time to concern themselves with the aesthetic niceties of the building, and it can only be hoped that the church offered them some spiritual comfort. They must have constantly wondered whether they would ever return to the world outside the moat that separated them from it, a moat that also served as a sewer.

If you go north from Porta Venezia, taking Corso Buenos Aires to reach Via Palazzi, and taking the third turning to the left, you can view what remains of the Lazzaretto, the church of San Carlo – of no great merit despite being the work of *Il Pellegrini* – and a section of the portico that forms part of the northern section of the school at No.12 Via Tadino, the first road crossed by Via Palazzi.

Going south down Corso Venezia, away from Porta Venezia and the Lazzaretto, you will reach the Planetarium, which lies within the public gardens. The Planetarium was built in 1929 in the style of a classical temple. It consists of one huge room with a hemispherical vault on which are displayed the stars and planets. Visitors take one of 600 revolving seats. Next along Corso Venezia is the Natural History Museum, housed in a pseudo-Romanesque building dating from 1893, although the collection was started earlier. Displays include vertebrates and invertebrates, minerals and fossils, and of special note is the collection of birds. Other rather exceptional items include a 40-kg topaz, a full-size Triceratops, a huge gorilla and an even bigger elephant. The section on Italian animals is particularly interesting to visitors intending to spend a day or two out of town.

Villa Reale Beyond the Natural History Museum turn right into Via Palestro in order to reach the Modern Art Museum housed in Villa Reale, a fabulous building in pure Neo-Classical style completed for the Count Ludovico Barbiano di Belgioioso and later bought by the Government of the Cisalpine Republic for Napoleon. Napoleon actually spent time at the villa, staying there with Josephine. After the Emperor had met his Waterloo, both Eugene di Beauharnais and Marshal Radetzky lived at the villa.

Visitors to the villa arrive at the front, to be greeted by a huge work by Marino Marini, and if they are not careful see only the

Villa Reale

front. This is a mistake. The back of the villa, which overlooks a last section of the gardens, is by far the best façade, especially if viewed across an acre of grass, or across the delightful duck pond at the bottom of the slope below the house. This façade is stupendous, a riot of columns, arched windows and reliefs of scenes from mythology. At each end there are set-forward wings, and the whole is topped by a stone balustrade and a row of statues.

The interior of the villa is largely taken over by the Modern Art Museum which is spread through 35 rooms that are still marvels of late eighteenth-century elegance, with luxurious decoration in plaster, parquet floors and chandeliers. The art collection concentrates on the effect of world movements on northern Italian painters of the nineteenth-century. Here, therefore, is the work of Lombard, Tuscan and Piedmontian artists in Impressionistic style. Much of the work will be new to English-speaking visitors as Italian painters have not 'travelled well', but there is much to admire. Certainly the work of Arturo

100

Left
One of the rooms of Villa Reale

Above
Marino Marini statue, entrance to Villa Reale

Tosi – who was born in nearby Busto Arsizio and died here in Milan – is superb, as is that of Sironi and Carrà. The sculpture of Medardo Rosso is also worth more than a passing glance.

To make comparisons easy there are works by the more famous artists in the Impressionistic field, Renoir, Dufy, Cézanne, Gauguin and Manet, together with later 'modern' works by Picasso and Matisse.

One section of the building holds the Marino Marini Museum, a collection of the art – sculpture, paintings and drawings – of the artist who completed the courtyard entrance work. The collection was donated to the museum in 1973.

The parkland at the back of the Villa Reale is separated by a fence from the Boschetti di Via Marina, the little wood of the Via Marina, an elegant tree-lined street designed by Piermarini but now thoroughly ruined by the car park of ACI, the Italian Automobile Club. Before the building of the street the local lime wood was famous as a recreation area.

Two Fine Palazzos Where the Via Palestro leaves Corso Venezia the visitor is close to two quite delightful *palazzis*. Palazzo Rocca-Saporiti, just across the street from Via Palestro, was built in 1812 to a design by the set designer of La Scala. It is elegantly Neo-Classical, although few other houses of the style have such enormous loggias, even though the loggia is such a feature of Italian architecture. This one has Ionic columns and a balustrade, and the man who suggested that it was well enough defined to classify as a speaker's gallery seems to have been right. At the top is a fine row of sculpted Roman gods. Palazzo Castiglioni stands across Corso Venezia and a little way down from Palazzo Rocca-Saporiti. It was built in 1903 with a façade in what the Italians could call Liberty style, but which we would call Art Nouveau. It is virtually one complete relief of figures and flowers, trees and shrubs. The overall effect is extraordinary. The architect's wish was to celebrate nature and in this Sgr Giuseppe Sommaruga succeeded admirably.

Not everyone was impressed, however. Originally on either side of the doorway there were statues of nude young ladies, languidly posed. Soon the statues had become famous – or perhaps, infamous

Palazzo Rocco-Saporiti

102

– the Milanese christening the house *Ca' di Ciapp* (the House of Buttocks'), to the great amusement of Sommaruga. The nudes became a favourite meeting place of young men, at which point the local wives and mothers could contain themselves no longer and insisted that they be moved elsewhere, much to the annoyance of the sculptor Ernesto Bazzaro. Today the girls stand in the courtyard of the Columbus Clinic in Via Buanarotti near the Fiera (Metro stops Buonarotti or Wagner, for those determined to see what all the fuss was about; purely in the interests of research, of course). They stand close to a wall, now partially covered with ivy.

Close to the palazzo there is a fine restaurant. Girarrosto, at No. 31 Corso Venezia (Palazzo Castiglioni is at No. 47) is Tuscan, which might seem a bit unreasonable in this, the capital of Lombardy. Such thoughts will not survive the eating of a Florentine steak. The restaurant is closed at lunchtime on Sunday and all day Saturday.

Palazzo del Senato From either Palazzo Castiglioni or the Boschetti di Via Marina it is not far to the Palazzo del Senato. The *palazzo* was built by Cardinal Federico Borromeo as a **Palazzo Castiglioni**

Palazzo Senato

headquarters for the College of Swiss Seminaries. It was begun in 1608 by Fabio Mangone and completed, after his death, by Francesco Maria Richini who was responsible for the elegantly curved façade. However, work progressed very slowly with many pauses for second and third thoughts, and the project outlasted not only Richini but the seventeenth-century. It was, in fact, completed only shortly before the College was moved elsewhere, the *palazzo* becoming a government building. Under the French it housed the senate (hence the name), and today it houses the State Archive, a collection of documents covering 1,200 years of Lombardian history, one of the most important archives in Italy.

Richini gave the façade a concave curve so that carriages could more easily approach the doorway. This is not only practical but the effect of the curve is also very pleasing, particularly after all the flat façades that have been passed to reach the *palazzo*. To the left of the doorway is the first postbox in Milan, dating back to the Napoleonic era.

Inside the *palazzo* there are two vast linked courtyards. They are occasionally the venue for outdoor sculpture exhibitions which give the visitor the chance to see not only some fine art, but also the courtyards themselves.

On the way back to Corso Venezia along the Via Senato the visitor passes San Pietro Celestino, a fourteenth-century church, once attached to a convent of the Benedictines of the Celestial Congregation. It was built of soft stone and has needed considerable renovation, some of it in cement, so that it is now almost pure, but delicate, rococo. The campanile dates from the first building and has a delightful bell loggia. Inside there is a fine painting of St Benedict by Camillo Procaccini.

Seminario Arcivescovile Go right along Corso Venezia again reaching to the left across the road, the Palazzo Fontana-Silvestri (see pages 128–9) one of the best buildings in Milan. Opposite the *palazzo*, on your side of the road, is the ornate and awesome entrance to the Seminario Arcivescovile, the Archbishop's Seminary. The two sculpted figures that flank the entrance symbolize holiness and wisdom (*la pietà e la sapienza*) and were completed in the mid-seventeenth-century by the sculptor Giovan Battista Casella. Apparently much amusement was caused when it was learned that the bill for the work was even more excessive than the shape of the statues.

The seminary itself is difficult to see, the approach from the road leading only to an imposing wall with faceless windows and a usually barred door. It was built by San Carlo Borromeo in 1564 and is square, the four walls enclosing a courtyard that measures 56 metres on one side and is surrounded by a double tier gallery, each floor of which is supported by double Doric columns. The colonnade supports the Borromeo family motto, *Humilitas* (humility).

Behind the seminary, in the Palazzo Morando-Attendolo-Bolognini, is the Civic Museum of Milan which houses pictures and memorabilia from the history of the city. Chiefly the

collection covers the period from the eighteenth-century until the early part of the twentieth-century and so covers the most interesting period in the history of the city. Some of the paintings of the city are fascinating for the changes they highlight. Look out for the girl, modelled in bronze by Giuseppe Grande, who symbolizes one of the 'Five Days'.

Also in the *palazzo* is the Museum of Contemporary History which covers the history of the city through the period from 1914-1945. There are newspapers and posters, photographs and mementoes but it must be said that a lack of Italian language will limit the appeal of the collection.

Finally, the *palazzo* is now the permanent home of the Ugo Marsia collection of marine art. This includes some fine prints of early sailing ships and a library of books on marine topics, pirates and folk stories as well as marine architecture. Among the better items is a superb painted figurehead.

Two More Palazzos Finally, head back towards the Duomo, passing on the way two interesting *palazzi*. Palazzo Spinola lies in Via San Paolo. It was built for a rich banker in the early sixteenth-century but is more renowned as the home of the Societa del Giardino, the oldest and most prestigious club in Milan which has used the *palazzo* since 1818. Some of the most renowned Italian artists and aristocrats, including Alessandro Manzoni and Stendhal, Count Cavour and Vittorio Emanuele II, have been members.

At the bottom of the same road is the elegant triple-tiered Palazzo Tarsis, built around 1836 for Paolo Tarsis and reckoned to be the finest example of Neo-Classical architecture in the city. When it was built it was a significant addition to the city's houses as it heralded the start of the restructuring that saw the completion of Corso Vittorio Emanuele II. Look especially for the frieze of statues on the upper tier.

Opposite
The entrance to the Seminario
Arcivescovile

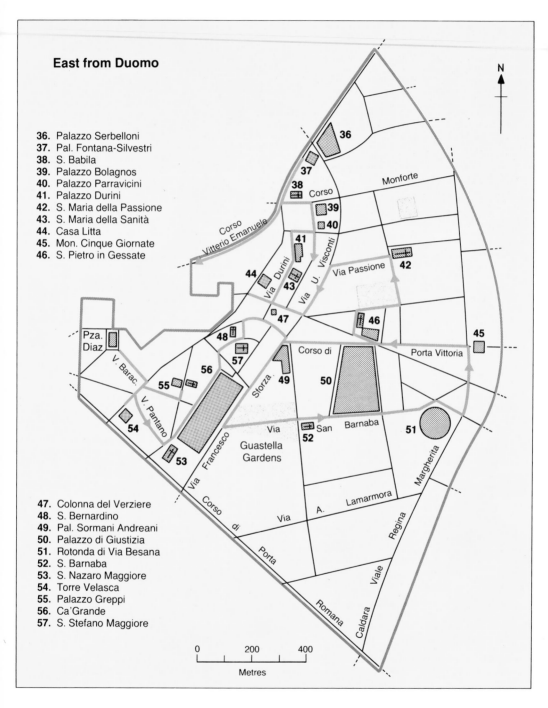

East from Duomo

36. Palazzo Serbelloni
37. Pal. Fontana-Silvestri
38. S. Babila
39. Palazzo Bolagnos
40. Palazzo Parravicini
41. Palazzo Durini
42. S. Maria della Passione
43. S. Maria della Sanità
44. Casa Litta
45. Mon. Cinque Giornate
46. S. Pietro in Gessate

47. Colonna del Verziere
48. S. Bernardino
49. Pal. Sormani Andreani
50. Palazzo di Giustizia
51. Rotonda di Via Besana
52. S. Barnaba
53. S. Nazaro Maggiore
54. Torre Velasca
55. Palazzo Greppi
56. Ca'Grande
57. S. Stefano Maggiore

Corso Monforte

Corso Vitterio Emanuele

Via Durini

Via U. Visconti

Via Passione

Pza. Diaz

V. Barac.

V. Pantano

Corso di Porta Vittoria

Porta Vittoria

Storza

Corso di

Via Francesco

Guastella Gardens

Via San Barnaba

Margherita

Lamarmora

Corso di Porta Romana

Regina

Caldara

Viale

N

0   200   400

Metres

Piazza Diaz

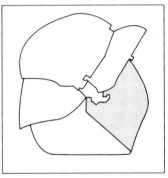

East from the Duomo Our trip around this part of the city defines a crude triangle, formed by Corso Venezia and Corso di Porta Romana, with Piazza del Duomo as its point. This is a widespread area with the real interest concentrated in the southern part, from the Ospedale Maggiore to the Rotonda. The northern part is also worth visiting though, and there are several excellent areas to rest and soak up the sun and the atmosphere.

Leave the Piazza del Duomo along Via Marconi, going past the Milan tourist office and reaching the Piazza Diaz with its ultra-modern, but truly delightful, monument to the *carabineri* by Luciano Minguzzi. Beyond, go out of the square by the left exit, Via Baracchini. Go right at the junction where Via Barracchini ends, then left into Via Chiaravalle and left again into Via Sant' Antonio to see the church of Sant' Antonio Abate. This was built in 1582 by the Teatini Fathers and took its name from a former church attached to a monastery of the Brothers of St Anthony, a curious horse-riding fraternity who 'kept alight the fires of St Anthony'. It is claimed that the church is one of the most complete examples of the Milanese baroque style, but I think the best feature is the campanile, the only part of the older building that remains. In brick, it is superb and rises above a cloister that is all that remains of the monastery. The cloister has

Torre Velasca.

three open arcaded sides and above it runs a gallery with a brick frieze along which winged griffins compete, each holding a shield with horse's heads. Elsewhere other assorted monsters complete the decoration.

Opposite the church is the Palazzo Greppi, an elegant Neo-Classical building dating from 1776. Its owner, Antonio Greppi, had social aspirations and spent much time and more money creating a fine façade and rooms so luxurious, and so dedicated to rich parties, that the city nobles came in droves. For a while the *palazzo* became an important meeting point of the political and

110

artistic halves of the city, but history does not specify whether in the longer term Sgr Greppi was admitted to the ranks of noblemen.

If instead of visiting the church and *palazzo* you continue across the piazza and into Via Velasca, your view is dominated, as any photograph taken south from the roof of the Duomo will be by the Torre Velasca. This tower was built in 1957 by local Italian architects, including Ernesto Nathan-Rogers. It is 106 metres high, its height not limited by technology, but by respect for the Madonnina on top of, the Duomo. The widening at the top is a tribute to the towers of the Sforzas, who were also fond of this sort of fungal shape. The name commemorates Don Juan Fernandez De Velasco, the Spanish governor of the city who, in 1598, allowed the widening of a local road so that the citizens could better celebrate their carnivals.

Basilica of San Nazaro Maggiore Go left before reaching the end of Via Velasca, following Via Pantano to the basilica of San Nazaro Maggiore. The basilica stands in a piazza named after the church, where there are also three small granite columns marking the entrance to the Vicolo Santa Caterina. These are all that now remain of a series of columns that surrounded the convent of Santa Caterina in the Middle Ages. The columns represented the start of sanctuary and many fugitives made their way there when the law threatened.

Also outside the church is a single column, the column of Sant' Ulderico, brought here when the Corso di Porta Romana was being reconstructed. The column is in the pink granite of the quarries of Baveno on the western shore of Lake Maggiore.

The basilica beside the columns is very ancient, one of the oldest in the city, founded in the fourth-century. That first foundation was called the Basilica of the Apostles, this being changed later to the Roman Basilica because of its position beside the Porta Romana. Only in 396, when Sant' Ambrogio had the remains of the saint brought to the city and placed in the church, did the name finally change to San Nazaro.

As with many of the city's churches, San Nazaro was gutted by fire in the early Middle Ages, when light could only be provided by open flames and work on roofs meant using braziers to melt lead. The rebuilding was in Romanesque style, although this work has now been lost behind a Baroque frontage with later

One who sought sanctuary was a Milanese noble called Landriani, who was pursued to the columns, but escaped inside the convent. The police, finally becoming fed up with being outwitted by the sanctuary laws, continued the chase inside, arresting the nobleman at the High Altar. The infuriated Milan Cardinal told the city governor that both the Chief of Police and the governor would be excommunicated if Landriani was not immediately released back to the convent. The governor had also had enough, however, and sent a message to the Cardinal saying that if the excommunication threat was carried out Landriani would be hanged outside the Bishop's Palace.

111

Neo-Classical additions. Recent renovation work has shown that beneath these modifications the fourth-century church is virtually complete.

One of the most interesting features of the building is the Trivulzio chapel through which the basilica is entered, its position on the original façade of the church having been responsible for the loss of the early, Romanesque, frontage. The chapel was started by Gian Giacomo Trivulzio to house his family mausoleum. Trivulzio was a *condottiero*, a general in a private army, and fought well and loyally for his Sforza duke, first against the French and then against the Venetians. For these considerable services he received nothing, his enemies using the time he was away to poison Francesco I Sforza against him, not least because they were jealous of the work on the chapel. Triculzo died in 1518, a worn-out man overcome by the injustices of life. Not for another two decades was his great work finished, and then only because a local artist, Bramantino, used his own cash to do it, believing the work to be a masterpiece. The tomb of Trivulzio bears a Latin inscription that, translated, reads, 'He who never found peace now rests – Silence'.

The basilica itself is in the form of a Latin cross with a single nave. Immediately on the right of the entrance, be sure to look through the small opening to catch a glimpse of part of the Romanesque façade which disappeared from view following work on the construction of Trivulzio's mausoleum/chapel in the early sixteenth-century.

Further on, near the eastern edge of the apse, is the little basilica (*basilichetta*) of San Lino, a very rare example of tenth-century pre-Romanesque architecture, also with a cruciform plan. This contains a stone, to the left of the altar, with an inscription that starts 'Ambrogio founded...'. Many believed that this means it is the foundation stone of the earliest basilica. Finally, look for the chapel of Sant Caterina that can be reached from the left transept. The chapel is mid-sixteenth-century and can also be reached from the Largo Richini. It has very recently been cleaned and restored, a work that was carried out with great care. The chapel should be visited to see the superb fresco showing the martyrdom of St Catherine painted by Bernardino Lanino in 1546. The artist put himself in the picture; he is the man with the black beard and cap.

112

Ospedale Maggiore The Largo Richini, an airy square, leads to a pleasant length, (but narrow width) of parkland that is used by early morning paper readers on Sundays, and by students on all days. To its right the bicycle stands delineate grass from walkway as you approach what is definitely the better side of what was the Ospedale Maggiore.

This huge old hospital is known by the Milanese as the *Ca'Grande*, or 'Great House', and was built by Francesco Sforza in 1456 as a way of bringing together in one place about thirty little hospitals which had grown up around the Porta Romana. The design was by the Tuscan architect Antonio Averulino, popularly known as Il Filarete, who produced two vast quadralaterals separated by a huge central courtyard and closed in by square porticos on two floors. Sadly, Il Filarete died before completing his masterwork which was taken up by the Milanese Guiniforte Solari. In fact, the work was never really completed, additions simply being made over many years as the need for extra wards arose. This lengthy period of building explains why it is

The Basilica of San Nazaro

113

Above
Detail of western facade of Ca' Grande

Right
The Western facade of Ca' Grande

possible to find such a diversity of architectural styles, brilliant work from the Tuscan Renaissance period being mixed with the Baroque pieces and sections in later styles.

To pay for the considerable expense of running the hospital, the directors of Ca'Granda offered portraits to any worthy donor, the portrait to be painted full face for a large contribution, profile for a much smaller one and in various degrees between the two. The portraits were hung outside the hospital on all feast days so that the Milanese could admire their benefactors and those portrayed could bask in the glory of it all. It was a good system for everyone except the artist, who was frequently offered a low rate for the job, then had his payment deferred, and sometimes had to battle for months to receive anything at all. One artist, in an attempt to fight the system, painted a benefactor on horseback, claiming double payment – one for the man, one for the horse. The directors considered this, and decided that one payment only was in order because, although they could find evidence of the donation by the man, they could find no

114

evidence of any donation by the horse.

The completed portraits now hang in the Quaderia dell'Ospedale Maggiore, and can be seen on occasions, for just a few weeks every other year as a rule. Ask at the tourist office for details.

That the building exists at all is a wonder, as it was very badly damaged in World War II. The Milanese took great pains over its reconstruction in order to properly reinstate the great courtyard that formed the heart of Il Filarete's dream. The courtyard is breathtakingly beautiful, although to have your breath taken away it is necessary to keep student hours, the entrance from the Via Francesco side being controlled at all times, while that on the Via Festa del Perdono side is open when the University is also open. The central square of the courtyard is laid with grass, and trees break up its outline, while the defining walls are two-storeyed and arcaded, the upper arcade being filled on symmetrical sides to create windows.

The façade on the Via Fiesta del Perdono is over 280 metres long, a continuous sweep of elegant porticoes and arched windows

The main courtyard, Ca' Grande

115

of red terracotta, separated by sculpted medallions. By contrast, the Via Francesco façade is straightforward, almost ordinary.

Today the hospital is part of the University, housing the senate and the Faculties of Arts and Law. It also houses part of the local hospital administration, a nice link with the past.

Piazza San Stefano North of Ca'Grande is the Piazza San Stefano. This is an odd square, the Baroque façade of the church to the saint and the rococo façade of the church of San Bernardino contrasting poorly with the modern buildings whose architectural qualities – if they exist at all – are fairly well hidden. Away from a purely stylistic assessment, the square has great merits, the presence of students locally (there is another section of the University here) having resulted in a range of fine restaurants, take-away delicatessens and sandwich bars which the visitor to the centre will find delightful for offering a real Milanese touch to the menu at an affordable price.

The basilica of Santo Stefano Maggiore – once known as Santo Stefano in Brolo, because when it was first built it stood in the middle of a field; through the field ran a stream which fed ponds in which toads croaked noisily enough in the mating season to affect the services – was begun in the fifth-century. Like many of the other city churches it was destroyed by fire in the eleventh-century, being totally rebuilt (on the same foundations) in Romanesque style over a period of two hundred years. Unfortunately, at the end of the sixteenth-century the whole façade was remodelled, as was the inside, and the local population was outraged. The campanile was saved but it soon became ruinous. A fund was set up for its restoration, but before the work could even be started the campanile collapsed. The locals believed that the collapse was in protest at the new building work, but that hardly seems fair. There were two victims of the collapse, a beggar and an old priest. When the priest was searched it was found that he was carrying his will, and that he had left money for the restoration fund. The present campanile is one of the better features of the building.

Later work completed the Baroque look, a Neo-Classical reshaping of the interior being the last work completed. In 1979 the church was closed for worship and now houses the Diocesan Archive.

Opposite
A corner of the main courtyard, Ca' Grande

Of interest near the entrance to the old church is a floor-mounted grate that protects the *Pietra degli Innocenti*, the Stone of the Innocents, on which, legend has it, the Roman Emperor Valentian executed four innocent court officials framed by jealous colleagues. Another reminder of Milan's bloody past is the inscribed stone that commemorates the murder near the spot of Galeazzo Mari Sforza. This member of the ducal family was stabbed in the neck on Boxing Day 1476.

To the north, (that is, to the left when viewing from the square) of Santo Stefano is the sanctuary church of San Bernardino, together with an ossuary, built in the twelfth-century to minister to patients of, and to take the dead from, the local hospitals. The chief of these was the Ospedale del Brolo, the 'hospital in the field', the same field in which the basilica stood, one of the hospitals that was amalgamated into Ca'Grande. The buildings were damaged by the fall of the campanile but rebuilt, just in time to be almost completely razed by fire. A second reconstruction took many years, perhaps not surprisingly.

The ossuary inside the sanctuary is square with a vaulted ceiling. A fresco that is barely visible because of the darkness of the interior, and the effect of smoke from centuries of candles burning in front of a statue of Our Lady of Sorrow, shows the Triumph of Souls and dates from the turn of the seventeenth-century. It adds a macabre touch to the bones from the hospital. When the piles were examined it was found that the bones of condemned men were also placed here, some of the skulls showing clear signs of decapitation.

The rear of the church overlooks the Piazza Fontana, back close to the Duomo. Go right along the Via Verziere, passing another delightful park to the right where the lunching office workers help dispel the gloom of the ossuary. The square ahead, Piazza Verziere, commemorates one of the city's best fruit and vegetable markets which was held here in the nineteenth-century. The column in the *piazza* is of Baveno granite and was set up where San Carlo Borromeo celebrated Mass during the plague of 1576. The plinth at the base was used as an altar, Mass being celebrated in the open so that people too afraid to move from their houses could benefit from the service. The site was used again during the subsequent plague in 1630. The present name of

The Colonna del Verziere

Colonna del Verziere is new, the column having once been the 'column of the cross' – after the statue of Christ holding an iron cross was added in the seventeenth-century – or 'of San Matroniano'. It is believed to be to a design by Il Pellegrini, although its actual construction was not until a century after the architect's death.

Piazza Verziere to the Rotonda East from the Piazza Verziere is the Palazzo Sormani-Andreani, on the high-angled junction of Via Francesco Sforza and Via Guastella. The *palazzo* looks so much like a 1950s cinema (or is it a small-town railway station?), with its curves and ornate super-structure, that it comes as a surprise to learn that it is seventeenth-century. Today it is the headquarters of the Milan Public Library and houses a vast collection of books, newspapers and periodicals. The historical interest of the collection and, indeed, of the *palazzo* itself has led to a decision to open it as a museum. By now this has probably happened, and the interested visitor will need to contact the tourist office for exact details of opening times.

119

Go down Via Francesco Sforza, and look out for the façade of the church of San Giovanni in Conca, the majority of what remains of a church that once stood in Piazza Missori. (For the rest of what remains *see* page 134.) The façade is Lombard Romanesque style, probably built in the thirteenth-century, and still contains the old doorway. The church that now stands behind the façade is Waldensian.

Further down the main road is the western end of the Giardino della Guastella, the Guastella Garden. The garden is the oldest, and many would say the most beautiful, of Milan's public gardens. Anciently it was the garden of the Guastella College. This college, renowned in its time, was built by the Countess Paola Ludovica Torelli della Guastella – thankfully, her name was

The fishpond, Guastella Garden.

120

shortened for the dedication – for the daughters of noble but impoverished families. The college was built by Il Pellegrini, but only the doors now survive. They can be seen at No.6 Via Guastella, a street named after the college rather than the other way around.

The highlight of the gardens is a wondrous Baroque fish pond that most definitely should be seen, even if there is occasionally just a little too much rubbish in the water. The rest of the garden is cool and shady, although the section across the Via San Barnaba is noticeable for its basketball courts which are far from shady and on which groups of young Milanese are frequently very warm. On the fish pond side, be sure to look for the small Neo-Classical temple, the work of Luigi Cagnola.

Along Via San Barnaba you will pass the church for which the street is named, another work by Galeazzo Alessi, although here he was enlarging and modifying an existing building. The façade is elegant, if ornate, with four statues in niches and much scrolling work. The interior frescoes include several works by Aurelio Luini. Also here is the tomb of San Saccaria, the founder of the Barnabites for whom the first church was built.

Detail of rear facade, Palazzo di Giustizia

Inside the Rotanda di Via Besana

Beyond, the street is sandwiched between the heavy rear façade of the Palazzo di Giustizia and the more delicate brickwork of the church of Santa Maria della Pace. The church was deconsecrated in the early nineteenth-century and converted into a warehouse, at which time its art treasures were moved out to the Brera where they still remain, despite the church having been reconsecrated in the twentieth-century. The *palazzo* itself will be dealt with later when the trip reaches its frontage, but it is worth a long look as you move past.

To the right at the end of Via San Barnaba is the Rotonda di Via Besana, one of the most delightful buildings in the city. The Rotonda is a large, simple brick structure, built in 1695 as a cemetery for the dead of Ospedale Maggiore. It was closed in 1782, after which there was an attempt to convert it into a Pantheon for the new Italy. This attempt failed and the Rotonda served time as a hospital for contagious diseases and as the Milan hospitals' laundry before becoming a permanent centre for exhibitions. The inside is a distinct change from the outside, with the walls porticoed in fine style and with a (now deconsecrated) chapel dating from 1713. On Sunday mornings the Rotonda is used by Milanese families who bring their children, secure in the knowledge that they will not be harmed by traffic and that the arcaded walkway is a good place to play. Here and there someone will be reading a newspaper. It really is a fine place to spend time.

Around Piazza Cinque Giornate On the eastern side of the Rotonda is the wide major road of Via Regina Margherita which leads to Piazza Cinque Giorante, the square of the Five Days, where stands the monument to the Five Days. The monument is the work of the sculptor Giuseppe Grandi and was completed in 1895 to celebrate the Cinque Giorante, the Five Days of Milan (18-22 March 1848). The bronze obelisk is 22 metres high and is decorated with the names of the dead of the Five Days together with a group of five weary people symbolizing both the period and the spirit of the Milanese. The latter is further symbolized in the awakening lion and the eagle that holds the emblem of the city in its feet. Beneath the monument, in a hundred urns, lie the victims of the battle.

The piazza is huge, and roads meeting there are wide and not easy to cross; you need one eye on the traffic, one on the trams and another on the tramlines to make sure they do not send you sprawling. You might wish to choose one of the square's bars and have a coffee and rest before risking a crossing to the monument itself. After, find Corso di Porta Vittoria and follow it westward to reach the frontage of the Palazzo di Giustizia.

What to say about this *palazzo*? The facts are that the Palace of Justice was built between 1935 and 1940 in a style that is known in Italy as Littoria, but which we would term Fascist. It is entirely faced with marble, over 30,000 square metres of it. It is functional rather than decorative, but does hold some important modern artwork, sculptures by Arturo Martini and frescoes by Gino Severini and Carlo Carrà, the latter an artist whose work is also seen in the Villa Reale. I am inclined to leave it at that. On first sight I thought the building the ugliest in Milan, but my opinion changed a little after seeing the Via San Barnaba façade, which is less sense-slaughtering and even has some redeeming features. Perhaps 'one of the ugliest buildings in Milan' might be more appropriate...

The church of San Pietro in Gessate.

123

Opposite the *palazzo* is the beautifully tree-lined framed Romanesque façade of the church of San Pietro in Gessate. Did they deliberately position the *palazzo* to make impolite comparisons easy?

The church is a much reworked building that began life in the sixteenth-century and is now having its interior restored to that period. The work has brought to life a number of fine frescoes which were concealed beneath a thick layer of plaster.

The church is Romanesque and approached along a tree-clad path that makes a very pleasant change from the more normal city approach – straight off the road. Inside there are three aisles and twelve side chapels. In those on the right there is sixteenth-century work by Antonio Campi, *Il Bergognone* and Aurelio Luini. On the left the frescoes in chapels two, four and six are attributed to the fine fifteenth-century artist Donato di Montorfano. The real treasure, however, is in the chapel of Sant' Ambrogio where Ambrogio Grifo was buried in 1493. The lid of his now-gone sepulchre remains, a marble piece with Grifo's carved effigy. The lid, in red and white marble is attributed to Antonio Busti, known as Il Bambaia, who was born in 1483 and died in 1548. Almost as good are the chapel frescoes, scenes from the life of Sant' Ambrogio by Bernardo Zenale and Bernardino Butinone.

When it was new the church was attached to a monastery, the cloisters of which can be still seen at the back (reached from Via Corridoni).

Santa Maria Della Passione Continuing along Via Corridoni you will reach Via Conservatorio to the left. Take this to the huge church of Santa Maria della Passione, the largest church in Milan after the Duomo and renowned for the art treasures it holds. It was founded by Daniele Birago who gave land for it and a monastery of Lateran Canons towards the end of the fifteenth-century. The tomb of the founder can be seen beside the door into the sacristy. Work on the church progressed slowly after its founding – the superb cupola was built in 1530 and the naves in 1573, while the façade was added only in 1692.

The façade is squat and heavy – the architect deliberately lowered it to allow a frontal view of the octagonal tiborium that surmounts the cupola – but it is difficult not to admire the effort

that must have gone into it. The tiborium itself is thought to be a masterpiece of Renaissance art, although it hardly seems to be in the same class as that on Santa Maria delle Grazie. Those who visit the church in late spring and early summer will be entranced by the swifts who have set up home in the upper reaches of the building and wheel about the place, filling the area with their raucous but comforting squealing.

The church of Santa Maria della Passione

Inside, the church is the shape of the Latin cross, with a plethora of side chapels. There are so many works of art in the church that it has been declared a museum and is included as such on the official list of Milanese museums. Much of the fresco work is by Daniele Crespi, including the scenes from the Passion on the columns that support the nave and octagon. Strangely, these scenes do not name the church as you might think; that honour goes to a fresco by an unknown sixteenth-century artist, the Madonna of the Passion, in the fifth chapel on the right. In the chapel in the left transept is a Last Supper, the work of Gaudenzio Ferrari, while on the altar of the chapel in the right transept is a

125

Deposition by Bernardino Luini. The sacristy has fine frescoes by Ambrogio da Fossano (known as Il Bergognone) and his son Bernardino.

From the front of Santa Maria della Passione go west, following Via Passione to Via Visconti. Go left to return to Piazza Verziere, exiting along Via Cavalotti. Ahead now, and then right, is Corso Europa in which stands the interesting Casa Litta – not to be confused with the even more interesting Palazzo Litta. The House of the Litta has a beautiful rococo doorway behind which is an even more beautiful Renaissance courtyard with porticoes supported on Doric columns. When foundations for the house were being dug – the house was built for the Marquis Litta in the sixteenth-century – Roman mosaics were discovered.

A little to the west of Casa Litta is the church of San Vito al Pasquirolo, a church in a more than usually pretty Baroque style that once stood in meadow land, its position explaining the name – 'San Vito in the pasture'. Today it stands less elegantly, surrounded by modern buildings which do their best to dwarf and ignore it. Mass is celebrated here at midday, the church having been reconsecrated after a long deconsecration period. Inside, the church has lost all its movable decoration, although the stucco work is interesting. Note too the Roman remains around the outside, the church having been built on the side of Roman Milan's Hercules Baths, one of the last pagan works completed in the third-century before the city became Christian.

Those not inclined to make the detour to see the Casa Litta will content themselves with turning right earlier, into Via Durini. Here, to the right, you will find the church of Santa Maria della Sanità, with its weird-looking façade. It has long been held to look like a cello, but the elliptical window above the door looks like a beak to me, so that with the round windows above the upper façade looks nothing so much as a chick wearing a Napoleonic hat. Further up the road stands the Palazzo Durini which, along with the Palazzo Annoni, represents the most beautiful example of a seventeenth-century private Milanese house. The façade is wonderfully elegant, the Baroque dressing being set off by superb windows. The *palazzo* is named after the rich merchant, Giova Battista Durini, for whom it was built. Unfortunately the orientation of the *palazzo* means that it gets very little sun to set it off; this together with the dark paint and stonework, means it looks rather sombre.

To Piazza San Babila At the top of Via Durini go right along Via Borgogna. To the right here is Via Cerva in which stands a restaurant named after one of Milan's ancient mortal enemies, Barbarossa. It is a fine place in a delightful old *palazzo*. It is incumbent upon you, should you choose to go there, at least to contemplate the idea of Risotto Barbarossa, or even the same gentleman's kidneys.

Piazza San Babila

Opposite Via Cerva is Via Cino del Duca in which you will find Palazzo Parravicini and Palazzo Bolagnos. The former is one of the best examples of early fourteenth-century architecture in Milan, even though it is a small house almost lost among the surrounding buildings. It was built for the Parravicini family, a family of noble birth from Brianza and has a fine, if dirty, façade of red brick and elegantly simple windows. Palazzo Bolagnos is almost as good, being a near-perfect example of a rococo house.

At the top of the street go left to reach Piazza San Babila and the church of the same name. San Babila is set on the ruins of a fourth-century church, and that itself was built on the foundations of a pagan temple to the sun. From across the square the Romanesque lines of the church are masked, not only by later work that was in the Baroque style, but also by the adjacent multi-floor modern buildings and the traffic lights, the latter set in such a position that no useful photograph can be taken that does not include them. The frontal view also misses the octagonal tower, one of the church's better elements, although it does catch the tall, slender campanile. It would be nice to find that the campanile is original Romanesque, but alas it is as modern as 1820, replacing the first that had long since collapsed.

Inside the church there is a plaque commemorating the baptism of Alessandro Manzoni on 8 August 1785, and a fine altar surround by Ludovico Pogliahi, who was responsible for the central doors of the Duomo.

On the opposite side from the campanile, and at the front of the church, is a column surmounted by a lion. The lion is a symbol of St Mark, but also of the Venetian empire, although whether either of these symbols is relevant here is not known with certainty. Some say the lion was set up to celebrate a victory

127

Palazzo Fontana-Silvestri

over the Venetians – although that seems barely credible, a defeated, down-trodden beast being the more usual symbol for a defeated enemy – others that it simply marks the position of the old eastern gate, through which travellers to and from Venice would go. It has also been pointed out that the ancient quarter of the city around the eastern gate took, as its own symbol, a black lion on a white background.

Along Corso Venezia Going north along Corso Venezia you reach Palazzo Fontana-Silvestri standing almost opposite the entrance to the Semanario Arcivescovile. The *palazzo* is a very rare example of a private house from the time of the Sforzas, and is attributed to Bramante. In its earliest history the building housed the guardian of the eastern gate, but it was taken over by the Fontana family and completely remodelled, a reshaping that was carried out with all the grace of Renaissance art. The façade is a delight, from the Tyrolian-like overhanging eaves down past the circular windows, the slender arched windows, the wrought iron balcony and even the odd chopped-off arches and remodelled square windows. To find such a delight in the middle of a modern street makes any trip worthwhile.

Further north along Corso Venezia is Palazzo Serbelloni, an enormous building in Neo-Classical style created in 1793 for Duke Serbelloni by the enlarging of a seventeenth-century *palazzo*, part of which can still be seen – the brick section in Via San Damiano. Napoleon Bonaparte, Metternich, Napoleon III and Vittorio Emanuele II all visited the house, and each must have been impressed by the colossal Ionic columns that hold up the façade and hem in the doorway. The Italian author Parini also spent time at the house, as tutor to the family children.

Back to the Duomo Our return to the Duomo is by way of Corso Vittorio Emanuele, a pedestrian-only street that is used as an outdoor art gallery, works by contemporary sculptors being erected at intervals along the length and changed regularly. The effect of the works, all with a backdrop of the Duomo itself, is stunning. Not so visually exciting, but of considerable interest from an historical point of view, is the statue of the Man of Stone at No.13. The statue was raised to the honour of Archbishop Adelmanno who died in 956. Originally it stood in a small church in Via San Pietrò which has long since disappeared, and was christened the 'Man of Stone' when it was repositioned. On the pedestal the chiselled inscription from Cicero reads, 'he who judges his neighbour should be free from all defects himself.' From the early nineteenth-century this inscription inspired the local wits and the statue was frequently used for posters commenting on local politics or politicians. The posters were fixed at night and the culprits were never caught – or, more likely, never looked for by a police force who enjoyed the joke as much as the rest of the city. One particularly good comment at the time, much appreciated by everyone – except the recipient I assume – was the card that read *Arciduca 6 1 0*, translated as 'Archduke VI, you (one) are nothing'. The statue is late Roman, the head of (it is assumed) Archbishop Adelmanno having been added at a later stage in what was believed to have been tenth-century style.

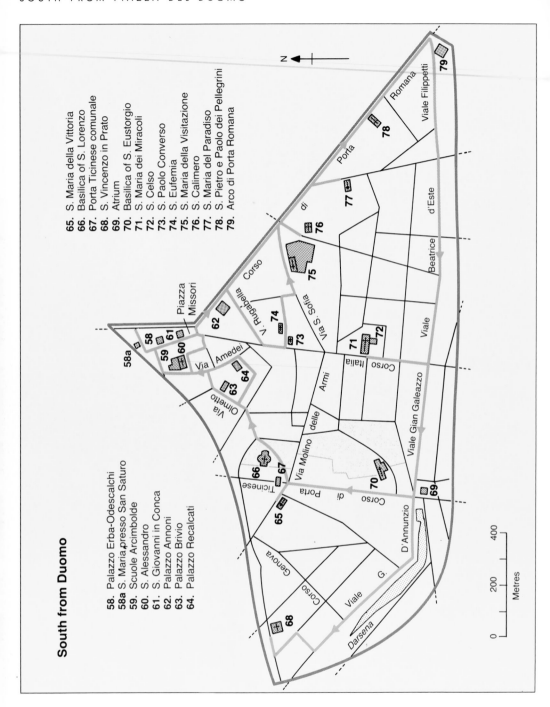

South from Duomo

58. Palazzo Erba-Odescalchi
58a. S. Maria presso San Saturo
59. Scuole Arcimbolde
60. S. Alessandro
61. S. Giovanni in Conca
62. Palazzo Annoni
63. Palazzo Brivio
64. Palazzo Recalcati

65. S. Maria della Vittoria
66. Basilica of S. Lorenzo
67. Porta Ticinese comunale
68. S. Vincenzo in Prato
69. Atrium
70. Basilica of S. Eustorgio
71. S. Maria dei Miracoli
72. S. Celso
73. S. Paolo Converso
74. S. Eufemia
75. S. Maria della Visitazione
76. S. Calimero
77. S. Maria del Paradiso
78. S. Pietro e Paolo dei Pellegrini
79. Arco di Porta Romana

130

South from Piazza del Duomo

Santa Maria Presso San Satiro The church of Santa
Maria presso (near) San Satiro is an awkward church for the
visitor, lying between two roads in such a way that a detour along
a busy shopping street is required to complete a visit. Still, the
busy street is home to one of the very few city-centre
supermarkets (a grand title for a relatively small shop, but it does
capture the flavour). If you are parched and need a large bottle of
something fizzy at a reasonable price as opposed to a small bottle
at an extortionate price, Via Mazzini is the place to go.

**Interior of the church of Santa
Maria presso San Satiro**

Santa Maria is a quite beautiful church, and one with a
fascinating list of unique features. The first church on the site was
built by Ansperto da Biassono, archbishop of Milan when the city
was part of the Carolingian empire. It was built in 876, and those
ancient parts of the church that remain are among the few
fragments from that time that still exist, not only in Milan, but
also in Lombardy. The archbishop dedicated the church to San
Satiro, the brother of Sant' Ambrogio. Of the earliest church the
major remaining section is an apse in the chapel of the Pietà,
although most of the chapel is from the rebuilding by Bramante
in the 1400s. The bell tower dates from the eleventh-century and
is the oldest in the Lombardy Romanesque style that still exists.

The Bramante building – it was the architect's first work in
Milan – is thought to be from the finest period of the Lombardy
Renaissance and is a masterpiece of space and depth, the more so
because of Bramante's superb use of a perspective fresco beyond
the High Altar. From the entrance to the church the fresco makes
the flat wall behind the altar look like an apse, and only when the
wall is approached is the illusion of curvature broken. Look too
for the cupola and arched ceilings that marry the high decoration
of Catholic churches with an excellent sense of style.

From the outside it is difficult to know whether to curse
Bramante's decision to demolish the original church – apart from
the internal apse structure and the (later) campanile, – or to
marvel at the soaring lines. The main, and best, façade, the one
seen from Via Torino from where the church entrance is reached,
was started by an earlier architect, but in an assumed battle
between the early man and Bramante the latter won the day,
completing the work seen today.

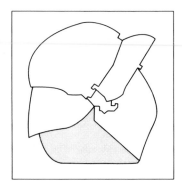

The reason for the odd name for the church, St Mary near St Satiro, is because of an ancient fresco of the Madonna and Child that stood over an external altar of the earliest (San Satiro) church. This fresco is mirrored by another that can be seen from Via Falcone at the back of the church. The story is told that on 25 March 1242 a 'man of vile condition called Massaccio' was walking in Via Falcone having, it is said, just lost all of his latest ill-gotten gains – 'vile condition' is a euphemism for criminal – at a local gaming house. One version of the story has Massaccio losing all of his clothes as well, which not only adds a new possibility to the origin of the saying 'to lose your shirt', but also a certain piquancy to the vision of the gambler outside the church. Massaccio was aggravated. Indeed, he is said to have been beside himself with rage and looking to pick a violent quarrel with anyone who happened along. No one did, so Massaccio attacked the fresco, stabbing at the neck of the Child Jesus. The 'wound' in the painting spurted blood all over the attacker. This miraculous event caused Massaccio immediately to repent his past life, and he became a Benedictine monk, dying at a great age with the reputation of having led a saintly life in his chosen monastery.

Not surprisingly, the Milanese were impressed by the miracle and over the years their offerings to the Madonna amounted to enough money to build a new church, the one that Bramante designed. The new church, although it incorporated the old

Piazza Guiseppe Missori

church of San Satiro, was named for the Madonna, which explains why the new church is known as Santa Maria presso San Satiro, the church of St Mary near St Satiro.

Having viewed the replacement external fresco and the church – although only through a haze of overhead tram wires – from the little square where Via Mazzini crosses Via Falcone and several other minor roads, go inside and see the real one which stands above the main altar, beneath Bramante's masterly pseudo-apse. A visit should also include the Chapel of the Pietà, occasionally known as the chapel of San Satiro, where there is a superb Deposition made up of terracotta figures by the artist Agostino De Fondutis. De Fondutis was also responsible for the brick frieze with cherubs in the sacristy.

Piazzas Giuseppe Missori and Sant' Alessandro

If a look at the Via Falcone end of the church is late in your visit, continue your walk by going south down the road, away from the church, to reach Via Unione. There go right to see the Palazzo Erba-Odescalchi, a sumptuous *palazzo* built by the Cusani family in the early 1500s, although it takes its name from a later Archbishop who used it as his palace in the eighteenth-century. The style is difficult to place, and is perhaps best describes as exuberant. Now go ahead to reach Piazza Giuseppe Missori, a square dominated less by the buildings, which are not well enough ordered to impose any discipline on the place, than by the statue of General Missori himself. He has been seated on his horse since 1916, when he was installed, contemplating a chaos he would never have allowed from his soldiers.

An alternative route to reach the square is to go right along Via Unione, then first left into Via Arcimboldi and left again into Via Lupetta to reach Piazza Sant' Alessandro. Just as you reach the square you will pass, to your left, the Scuole Arcimbolde, a huge building adjacent to the church of Sant' Alessandro. This school was built in 1609 and run by the Barnabites who were also responsible for the church. Giuseppe Parini, famous throughout Italy, but not elsewhere, was a pupil of the school; he was born near Lake Pusiano to the north of the city. It would appear from records at the school that Parini was not an inspired scholar.

The fine, Baroque-domed church after which the square is named was built in 1602 on the site of an earlier ninth-century temple. The façade is on two levels, the lower one with Corinthian columns in a contrasting colour that adds to the general attractiveness. The façade is flanked by symmetric towers. Inside there is a black marble stone with an inscription stating that entombed below are the remains of Bernabo Visconti transferred from a neighbouring church which was demolished. Regina della Scala, who built the church that gave the name to La Scala and was the wife of Bernabo, is also buried here. Elsewhere, the church has some excellent frescoes, especially the Life of the Saint, and the work of such artists as Daniele Crespi and Camillo Procaccini.

On the opposite side of the piazza from the church, beyond the row of elegant short pillars and the less fetching white domes erected to stop the Milanese from parking on the pavements, is Palazzo Trivulzio, a sixteenth-century building that has been remodelled and is in need of a little loving care. The son of the Marquis after whom the *palazzo* is named was the founder of the library that bears the family name – the Biblioteca Trivulziana – and is now housed in the Sforza Castle. When the collection was still in the *palazzo* (it was moved about 60 years ago) it was the most important private library in Milan. It was also one of the biggest, with over 70,000 books as well as a large collection of manuscripts and some ancient parchments.

In Piazza Missori, whichever route you have taken to reach it, are the ruins of San Giovanni in Conca, whose repositioned façade you have seen elsewhere (*see* page 120). The remains are of the apse and crypt of the historically well-known Romanesque Lombard church, and they stand incongruously between more modern structures. The church was demolished towards the end of the last century when the new road was laid down, and only the rescued façade was wholly retained. The crypt that remains here is thought to be the best-preserved Romanesque crypt in Lombardy and contains remains from paleo-Christian times through to the Renaissance. The vault is held up by ten small columns.

Piazza Sant' Eufemia Leave Piazza Missori along Corso di Porta Romana, heading back towards San Nazaro, but first stopping to admire Palazzo Annoni, to the left just before Via Velasca is reached. This house and Palazzo Durini (*see* page 126) are believed to be the first two town houses to have been built in the city after the population had been decimated by plague in

1630, when, it it thought, as many as 70,000 Milanese died. The *palazzo* therefore represents the height of architectural fashion for the mid-seventeenth-century, and was at the centre of the post-plague reawakening of city life.

After the *palazzo* take the next road to the right, Via Rugabella, and follow this to the Corso Italia. Go left to reach the small square of Piazza Sant' Eufemia, where across a small lawn that is longer than it is wide and bordered by tall conifers, you will see the church that gives the piazza its name. The church is in Romanesque style, but in this case it is mock-Romanesque, completion being many years after the style had ceased to be used. Although the chalk and brickwork is striking, the over-elaborate design is indicative of a later period of construction. Internally, Sant' Eufemia is pleasant rather than exciting, although the large altar piece, by Marco d'Oggiono, a follower of Leonardo and one of the supporters of his monument in the Piazza della Scala, is excellent.

Across from Sant' Eufemia is the more sombre church of San Paolo Converso, set behind a seventeenth-century column – sometimes named after San Senatore, sometimes after Sant' Eufemia – topped by the saint himself. The church was built in mid-fifteenth-century as a convent church for a now long-gone convent. San Paolo was deconsecrated many years ago, and its huge interior is now used as an art gallery. Some of the external marble work is superb, although the overall effect is a little too sombre for easy viewing.

San Calimero Church Take Via Sant' Eufemia up the side of the church of Sant' Eufemia, as the view of the rear end of the church is very good. Turn right into Via San Senatore and go left when this ends at Via Santa Sofia. On the right side of this road is Santa Maria della Visitazione, the church of St Mary of the Visitation. The original church here was taken over as a convent church when San Carlo Borromeo set up the convent for girls who had been orphaned by the plague. The convent was in the protection of St Sophia and the church was dedicated to her, but changed its dedication when the building was taken over by the nuns of the *Salesiane della Visitazione* order. In time the nuns remodelled the church so that it is now Neo-Classical. The façade is dominated by a statue of the Virgin, but the best feature is the courtyard, still flanked by

The fresco above the doorway of the church of San Calimero

A pinnacle on the facade of the church of San Calimero

sections of the original convent. The interior of the church is disappointing.

Beyond the church go right into Via San Calimero to reach a church that is far less disappointing. The first church here is believed to have been built in the fifth-century on the site of a pagan temple to Apollo. Some of the later remodelling work was done by Francesco Maria Richini, although what we now see is in Romanesque style, even though it post-dates the period by many years. The pinnacles on the façade top are especially good. Although the façade is not true Romanesque, the campanile most certainly is, as is the doorway of the *canonica* (the best translation is 'rectory', although in Italian the house of a priest is actually called the presbytery). The doorway is a very rare specimen, its arch a double layer of brick separated by a thin layer of Angera stone. The only other example of such a doorway in Milan is on the Palazzo Radice-Fossati. From the courtyard of the rectory to the right are fragments of old tombstones, some of Roman origin which suggest a one-time use of the area as a cemetery.

The interior of the church – reached by going through an ornate entrance archway that seems to be competing with the presbytery doorway for the eye of the visitor – has some good frescoes, particularly the Crucifixion with the Virgin and St John the Baptist by Giovan Battista Crespi, and a canvas study of the Nativity by Marco d'Oggiono. To the right of the altar is the ancient well-head into which, according to tradition, San Calimero was thrown by pagan priests after having been stoned.

Two Lesser-Known Churches Return to Corso di Porta Romana by going back up Via San Calimero, and go right to see two churches that are little visited. Go right into Corso di Porta Vigentina to visit Santa Maria del Paradiso, the church of St Mary of Paradise. The church took its name from that of an older church a little way off that was demolished to make way for the ramparts of the Porta Romana in 1532. The 'new' church was built in 1482. Along with the name came the Servite Fathers who had officiated at the old church. Under Napoleon these fathers were disbanded and the church came under the governorship of the more important building to San Calimero.

The façade is late Renaissance, with friezes and statues in fine style. Note that there is no campanile – very unusual. There was one, but the Austrians had it reduced in size because they believed that it might be used as an observation tower by the recalcitrant Milanese. Strangely, it was later used for the first city telegraph! Later again, it was demolished altogether.

Inside the church, fixed in front of the presbytery, there is a circular stone with a hole at its centre. On 13 March each year a wooden cross is placed in the hole. The ceremony is said to derive from the day in the year 52 when San Barnaba did the same thing outside the walls of Milan to symbolize the city's conversion to Christianity.

Back on Corso di Porta Romana continue eastward to reach the second church, San Pietro e Paolo dei Pellegrini, the church of Saints Peter and Paul of the pilgrims. The church gets its name from the adjacent hospice where pilgrims on their way to or from Rome once stayed. The hospice was closed in 1770 and pulled down. The church is noticeable for its dowdy appearance, the barely visible fresco of St Peter in the circle above the door and its general air of being run down. At one time there were fine frescoes inside by pupils of Giotto, but even these have gone. So why bother to come? There are two reasons: firstly, in the summer of 1990 major work started on the church which could restore it to something like its original form; this would make it interesting, because pilgrim churches are rare. Secondly, its position, hard up against a modern building, and beside and across from many more, demands attention. The little church has suffered from the rigours of time and town planning, normally a lethal combination, and survived. For that it deserves a little of everyone's time.

Twin Churches To continue, take Via dei Pelligrini, the Pilgrim's Road, or, better still, continue along Corso di Porta Romana to Piazzale Medaglie d'Ora where the old arch of the Porta Romana itself stands. The arch of Porta Romana ai Bastioni, to give it its full title, was built in 1598 to commemorate Margherita of Austria leaving the city on her way to marry Philip III of Spain, although the ramparts into which it was fitted had been erected half a century before. It is a triple arch of somewhat sombre appearance despite the elegant decoration of friezes and figures. Nevertheless it is widely believed to be the finest of all the remaining gates of the Spanish walls.

To continue your journey, follow the line of the old bulwarks, taking Viale Flippetti, and then Viale Beatrice d'Este and Viale Gian Galeazzo beyond, westward (right) along the old line. This route would lead to the Porta Ticinese in Piazza XXIV Maggio, the Square of 24 May, but deflect at Corso Italia, and follow that road back into the city to visit the twin churches of San Celso and Santa Maria dei Miracoli.

The church of San Celso, now standing somewhat forlornly beside the bigger, more illustrious church, has the longer history. On this site Sant' Ambrogio built a basilica in the fourth-century, but that early church was replaced in the tenth-century by the Milanese Archbishop Landolfo II. Landolfo's new church had a Benedictine monastery attached to it and a hospice opposite for orphans, the little Children of San Celso. A Baroque façade was added in the seventeenth-century but much of this was lost when it was suggested that it was shadowing the more important church of Santa Maria beside it. The new pseudo-Romanesque façade maintained only the doorway. The beautiful campaniole, behind and to the right, is real Romanesque.

Through the fifteenth-century wooden door there is little to detain the visitor, just a few tantalizing traces of eleventh-century frescoes.

The church beside San Celso is, technically a shrine, *Il Sanctuario di Santa Maria dei Miracoli presso San Celso.*

At the end of the fourth-century a search organized by Sant' Ambrogio discovered the remains of the martyrs San Nazaro and San Celso in this part of the city. Sant' Ambrogio transferred the remains of San Nazaro to the basilica that now bears his name, raising a second basilica here for the remains of San Celso; that basilica was replaced by a church. On an outside wall of this was painted a Madonna and Child. Some versions of the miracle story actually attribute the fresco to Sant' Ambrogio himself, although there is little hard evidence for the saint having been an artist. Over the centuries this painting acquired a reputation for being miraculous, although in an ill-defined way, so that in 1413 Duke Filippo Maria Visconti decided to build a church to house the work and shelter it from the weather. In this new church, on 30 December 1485, while plague was sweeping through the city, a crowd gathered at the church to ask help of the Madonna. As

Facade of the church of Santa Maria dei Miracoli

they watched, the image of the Madonna moved, making signs of comfort and hope. From that day the plague began to abate, and to show its gratitude the city decided to build a new church. Money poured in and work began in 1493 although it was to be a century before the work was completed; this timescale explains the stylistic variation of the church, with elements of both Renaissance and Baroque architecture.

In front of the church is a four-sided courtyard, porticoed in red brick on three sides and with the façade on the fourth. The façade is beautiful, in white marble with height and elegance. Some might accuse it of looking like a wedding cake, but I would suggest it has just the right amount of decoration. There are four tiers, with wings over the courtyard porticoes that are crowned by obelisks. At the top the Virgin is flanked by angels. On the first tier are the figures of Adam and Eve, while on the second a fine relief of Christ's birth is flanked by figures of the Annunciation, the presentation at the Temple and the Magi. On the third tier are Jeremiah and Ezekiel.

Inside there is more marble, – the marbled floor is very good – but it is for its art that the interior is famous. The paintings are virtually priceless, covering three centuries of Lombard devotional work up to the start of the Neo-Classical period, and the

Detail of facade of the church of Santa Maria dei Miracoli

decorative work is exquisite. The paintings include works by both Camillo and Giulio Cesare Procaccini, by Il Bergagnone and Annibale Ferrari. The painting of the Virgin blessing Christ before the Passion by Urbino was once popular with newly-wedded couples who knelt before it and asked for a blessing on their marriage.

The third chapel on the right is called the Crucifixion chapel because it contains a wooden crucifix carried in procession by San Carlo Borromeo during the time of the plague of 1576. At the head of the left transept is a very early Christian sacrophagus which held the remains of San Celso until, in 1935, they were transferred to the Crucifixion chapel. On the sarcophagus are carved scenes from the Old and New Testaments.

In the second chapel of the left aisle is another miraculous painting, a fourteenth-century fresco of the Madonna with Child called the Madonna of the Tears because it was seen to cry on 13 July in 1620, perhaps as an omen of the plague. The original miraculous Madonna of the name is to the left of the high altar, protected beneath finely-worked silver slabs. It, too, is a shrine for newly-weds.

The church is also famous for its sculpture, both statues and the presbytery altar with its rare marbles and gold-faced bronzes. The choir stalls beyond are excellent. Finally, in the treasury of the sanctuary is the Cross of Chiaravalle, a processional cross from the Abbey of Chiaravalle given to the church in 1296 by Ottone Visconti, Archbishop of Milan. The cross is a masterpiece of red jasper, gold, gilded silver and jewels and dates from the eleventh or twelfth-centuries. It is attributed to Benvenuto Cellini. Sadly, it is rarely on public display.

The Darsena Continuing along the line of the old ramparts you arrive beside the huge atrium in the Piazza XXIV Maggio. This huge monumental arch was erected in the early years of the nineteenth-century to celebrate the victories of Napoleon, although it was swiftly re-dedicated to Peace when the Austrians returned. This story will seem strangely familiar when we reach the Arch of Peace! The frieze at the top is inscribed *Paci Populorum Sospitae*, To the people's liberty and peace. The cost of the arch was met by Milanese nobles. West of the atrium is a large expanse of water popularly known as the port of Milan. The pool

Atrium, Piazzale XXIV Maggio

Winter market, near the Darsena

– more correctly known as the Darsena – was dug at the start of the seventeenth-century, during the time of Spanish domination of the city, and was connected to the twelfth-century canal which, by excavated waterway and river, connected the city with Lake Maggiore. For about six hundred years the port, (or the earlier, less grand version, known as the *Laghetto di Sant' Eustorgio*, the little lake of Sant' Eustorgio, in roughly the same spot) was used to deliver marble for the Duomo from the Visconti quarries at Candoglia in the Val d'Ossola which ends at Lake Maggiore. By river and canal the stone was brought to the port, from where it was hauled the short distance to the Duomo. Today the pool is used as a backdrop for fairs, with tents between the water's edge and the Viale Gabriele d'Annuzio, and floating rafts with bands. On the other side, along Viale Gorizia, there is a morning market. If you have the time the line 2 (Green line) metro to Porta Genova in the early morning, particularly if your trip to Milan is in the winter, and walk the short distance to the Darsena. As the sun comes up, a light mist rises from the water, softening the focus on the buildings in Viale Gabriele d'Annunzio and shrouding the heavy arch of the atrium. It is a romantic vision: Milan can never be Venice, but at such times it can also never be anything but Italian.

San Vicenzo in Prato From the north-western end of the Darsena it is a short step – cross Piazzale Antonio Cantore and go right into Via Daniele Crespi, then left into Via Sesto and right

June water fair on the Darsena

into Via San Calcero – to the church of San Vicenzo in Prato.

In his writings Sant' Ambrogio occasionally made reference to the Basilica Vetus, a very early (perhaps the earliest) Christian church in Milan. Some scholars have claimed that the fact that Ambrose did not give an exact site for the church – indeed, it seems he was actually careful *not* to – means that it was not a real church at all, merely a metaphor. Nevertheless, archaeologists and historians have looked for Vetus for years. Many believe that it lies under the church of San Vincenzo in Prato, even though there is no historical record of the church before the year 806.

San Vincenzo in Prato is the only Milanese example of a Pre-Romanesque church which preserves the early Christian plan of Roman basilicas. Despite this claim to fame the church has been subjected to several indignities, having been deconsecrated and used as a barracks and a chemical store before being reopened for worship in 1899.

Externally, the church is a simple and dignified brick structure, its lack of decoration suggesting a very early constructional date. Inside, the roof is of an equally early design. The campanile, and the octagonal baptistery to the left of the church are modern.

Basilica of Sant' Eustorgio

**External pulpit, Basilica of
Sant' Eustorgio**

Basilica of Sant' Eustorgio Following Corso Italia citywards (north) away from the atrium brings you to one of the highlights of a visit to Milan, the Basilica of Sant' Eustorgio.

Sant' Eustorgio ranks behind the Duomo and Sant' Ambrogio in importance as a religious building in Milan. The present structure dates from the ninth-century, although it has been much renovated, and was built on the ruins of a preceding church built by Bishop Eustorgio in the first quarter of the fourth-century. It is also said to be the spot where St Barnabas, who lived at the time of the Apostles, erected the first baptismal font in the city. Sant' Eustorgio built the church to house relics of the magi which, legend has it, he was given by the Emperor Constantine. When Milan was sacked by Barbarossa the relics were taken to Germany where they still rest, in Cologne Cathedral.

Recent renovations have recovered much of the original look of the church, and have discovered the remains of a vast and early Christian burial site, believed to be as early as second-century, and possibly even first-century. This is by far the earliest such site in Italy, and has become known as the Milan Catacombs. The campanile is twelfth-century, and the clock was added in 1306; it was Milan's first clock, but that on the church of San Gottardo was the first to strike the hours. Equally noticeable from the outside, on the left side, is a marble pulpit erected in 1597 to replace a wooden one used by St Peter the Martyr to preach against heresy. In 1252 St Peter was murdered by the heretics he sought to convert and is buried within the church.

Inside the church, virtually every chapel has something good to see. The first chapel on the right is Capella Brivio, built in Romanesque style in 1484, and named after the Marquis Brivio whose mausoleum it holds. The fresco of the Madonna and Child between St James and St Henry is by Il Bergagnone.

The Torelli chapel, the second on the right, is in Lombard Gothic style, dating from 1416. Its tomb is of Pietro Torelli.

The third chapel is of the Madonna of the Rosary, erected in 1464 but remodelled in 1733. The painting of the Virgin of the Rosary with Saints is by Camillo Procaccini.

The Capella Visconti is next, perhaps the second most important chapel in the church. It was built in 1297 by Matteo I Visconti, although the tomb is of a later member of the family,

Stefano, and his wife, Valentina Doria. The relief structure on this is superb, the Madonna being attributed to Giovanni di Balduccio of Pisa. The fine frescoes are fourteenth-century. They were covered with plaster in the seventeenth-century, but have now been successfully uncovered. Opposite the Visconti tomb is a crucifix painted on wood. This was known as the Lord of the Fever by the Milanese, and was especially good at giving comfort to sick women who would be brought here for the purpose.

The Capella di San Vincenzo Ferrari is the fifth chapel on the right. Although this has some good stucco work, most visitors will move on to the chapel of St Thomas, the sixth on the right. This was built in 1297 and holds the tombs of Gaspare and Uberto III Visconti. The canvas of St Thomas is by Camillo Procaccini.

Beyond the Torriani chapel, seventh on the right and dating from 1277, is the chapel of the Magi. The Roman sarcophagus here is where the remains of the Magi rested until the Bishop of Cologne, Reinhold Von Dassel, removed them in the wake of Barbarossa's victory. The remains have never been returned, except, that is, for one piece which is kept in the urn in the niche to the left of the sarcophagus. The marble triptych is believed by

**Interior of the Basilica of
Sant' Eustorgio**

some to be by Giovanni di Balduccio, although others believe it to be the work of one of the famed, but anonymous, masters from Campione. Another attribution to the Pisan master Balduccio is the section of a Visconti tomb below the altar table. The fresco of the Adoration of the Magi is equally attributed to Il Bramantino and Bernardino Luini.

In the presbytery the marble polyptych has scenes from the Passion and of saints and apostles. The fresco behind the altar, of Saints Dominic and Thomas among Angels is by Gaudenzio Ferrari.

In the pseudo-crypt below the choir are the uncovered remains of what may be parts of the original fourth-century church, together with a collection of other excavation finds.

The Portinari chapel was built in 1462 by a Florentine banker, Pigello Portinari, specifically to house the tomb of St Peter the Martyr and is thought to be the most beautiful Renaissance chapel in Milan. Some experts believe the chapel was the work of an 'imported' Florentine architect, but others see the hand of the Milanese Il Filarete. The rectangular chapel is roofed by a magnificent cupola decorated in coloured terracotta, with dancing angels by Antonio Amadeo. Much of the remaining fresco work is by Vincenzo Foppa, and the chapel is widely believed to be his masterpiece. In the centre of the chapel is Giovanni di Balduccio's superb tomb.

On 6 April 1252 Pietro di Verona, a Brother of the Dominican monastery of Sant' Eustorgio, where he preached vigorously against heresy, was murdered on the road from Como to Milan by killers hired by the heretics. As he lay dying, Pietro scratched the word *credo*, I believe, in the dust of the road. Soon the dead Brother was renowned as San Pietro Martire, St Peter the Martyr. Ironically, one of the assassins sought, and received, sanctuary at the monastery of Sant' Eustorgio.

The highly ornate white marble tomb has a sarcophagus with bas-reliefs of the saint's life, and a canopy supported by caryatids representing the four cardinal and the four theological virtues. At the top, the statues of Christ and the Virgin represent the Glory of Paradise. In the small chapel to the left of the tomb is the silver urn holding the skull of St Peter. One interesting finale to the story of the saint's head is that on 29 April each year some

After his murder the body of San Pietro was placed in a coffin in the left nave of the church of Sant' Eustorgio, but in 1335 it was transferred to a new, more elaborate sarcophagus sculpted by Giovanni di Balduccio for Giovanni Visconti and his nephew Azzone. In transferring the body of the saint, Giovanni Visconti managed to knock the head off and this he kept. Soon after he was struck down by terrible and mysterious head pains, which disappeared only after he had returned the head to the Dominicans. To make amends Giovanni had made a silver urn in which to keep the skull. Later the skull was transferred to a new urn commissioned by Ludovico il Moro, and this, together with the Balduccio tomb, was moved to a new chapel.

Milanese visit the Portinari chapel in order to touch their heads on St Peter's sacophagus, thus ensuring a year free of headaches.

Outside the Portinari chapel a staircase leads to the Milan Catacombs, with early Christian and some pre-Christian tombs. Finally, outside, to the left of the sacristy, are the remains of the old convent of Sant' Eustorgio, once the headquarters of the Inquisition, but destroyed by a combination of fighting between French and Spanish troops and the bombings of 1943.

Basilica of San Lorenzo Via Porta Ticinese North of Sant' Eustorgio, a little to the left when the Poreta Ticinese is reached, is another reminder of the Barbarossa destruction that resulted in the loss to the city of the remains of the Magi. Santa Maria della Vittoria was named for the victory over Barbarossa at the battle of Legnano, although the style is not from that time, being Baroque. The campanile is seventeenth-century and is a delight, finishing with a little onion dome cupola. Inside there is a fine fresco of the Pentacost by Camillo Procaccini.

The huge Baroque doorway to the left of the church once led to the Dominican monastery that stood beside the church. Today it leads to a greenhouse. Excavations on the site in the 1930s revealed that the Roman arena stood here. The arena was comparable in size to that at Verona, and was built in the first or second-century AD. It is believed that very little remains of the arena because it was used as a convenient quarry when the Basilica of San Lorenzo was being built.

Porta Ticinese is one of only two of the six gates that once pierced the Medieval city wall, built with a single arch rather than two; the two small side arches were only cut as an afterthought. The crenellations that top the gate are also recent, having been added in 1861 for no purpose other than appearance when the gate was given a facelift. The bas-relief on the outside is original fourteenth-century and attributed to the Pisan artist Giovanni di Balduccio. It depicts the Virgin together with the city saints, Ambrogio, Lorenzo, Eustorgio and Pietro Martire. Today a good photo of the gate can be spoiled by the tram wires that criss-cross the sky at this busy interchange; still, perhaps the city trams clattering through the gate are more satisfying than cars would be.

Through the gate are the Colonne di San Lorenzo, and the church itself. The sixteen Corinthian columns are the most

On 22 August 1629 the citizens of Milan watched as their Spanish governor Gonzalo Fernandez di Cordova went through the gate into exile from the city. Three years before the Spaniard had arrived in better circumstances as the new governor and captain general. Mismanagement on a grand scale resulted in a recall, and as the ex-governor left, the Milanese heaved a sigh of relief – and a good deal of rotten fruit and vegetables. Indeed, so much produce was thrown that the market of the Verziere was short of supplies for several days... or so the story goes.

conspicuous and obvious remains of Roman Milan, once part of a second-century AD pagan temple (probably to Cibele), but moved to the site in the fourth-century when construction started on the first Christian church to San Lorenzo. The columns are topped by a marble architrave that is interrupted at the half-way point by a brick arch. Of the two end arches the more delicate, southern one is fifth-century while the heavier northern one is Medieval.

Ideally you should approach the basilica of San Lorenzo from the east so that the full flavour of its construction can be appreciated. It is less a church, more a small town, a collection of octagonal and

Porta Ticinese

rectangular 'outhouses' each topped by a matching tiled roof. Buried within this township, but rearing up above it, is another octagon, a white marble addition finished with an elegant sugar-bowl lid of streaked copper. This trip leaves that fine view until later.

Interestingly, a tale from the tenth-century suggests that the idea of San Lorenzo resembling something other than a church is not new. Around 925 the Swedish duke Burcardo came to Milan as an ambassador for the German General Rodolfo di Borgogna, seeking to gain the support of the Milanese Archbishop Lamberto for the general to be made King of Italy. The duke stopped at San Lorenzo, which then stood outside the city walls, and commented in German to his companions that it appeared adequate to the task of holding the city by bay. Further on he suggested that there might well be a need to hold the basilica in order to subdue and imprison the Milanese if they tried to prevent the general's progress. All this conversation was in German, but fortunately, the story goes, there was a street urchin in the crowd watching the duke's procession who understood the language. He raced to the Archbishop's house to tell him what he had heard. The Archbishop greeted the duke most amiably, and suggested that they go hunting in the walled park reserved for the prelate and his special guests. The duke was delighted and readily agreed. The historian Liutprando who tells this story does not say whether the duke caught many in the hunt, but he does say that one late victim was the Swede himself whom Lamberto had tied up after the chase and roasted over a slow fire.

The basilica was built between the years 355 and 372 just outside the Roman city walls. Originally Arian, the church was converted to Catholicism in the fifth-century by Sant' Ambrogio who had a new chapel added on the left side. Since then the church has had a sad history, being gutted by fire in 1071, 1120 and 1124. After the last fire it was renovated in Romanesque style, but even then its misfortune was not over because in 1573 the central section collapsed. The architect Martino Bassi was engaged to rebuild the centre, and it was he who added the marble cupola.

The doorway of the church is defended by a monumental bronze of the Emperor Constantine, a copy of the Lateran statue and erected in deference to the Emperor's Edict of Milan in 313 which gave religious freedom to Christians.

The Colonne di San Lorenzo

151

Emperor Constantine's statue at the Basilica of San Lorenzo

The layout of the basilica differs from that of other Paleo-Christian churches because of its original Arian usage and comprise a large octagonal space with two sets of arcades, the large central cupola space and delightful niches setting off the ambulatory around its edge. There is also a woman's gallery reached by a staircase and decorated with ninth-century frescoes.

Today the walls of the basilica are bare, little trace remaining of the marble and golden mosaics that covered them in the fourth-century. The simple, dignified appearance that this lack of decoration gives is reinforced by the High Altar which, while being in Baroque style, is elegant rather than overly ornate. One exception to this rule of no decoration is a fine canvas by Aurelio Luini, son of Bernardino, in the ambulatory to the right of the entrance. The original chapels of Sant' Aquilino and Sant' Ippolito, and the chapel to San Sisto added by Sant' Ambrogio are exquisite, as is some of the art within the basilica. The mosaics in the chapel of Sant' Aquilino are especially fine, dating from the fourth-century. The mosaic of Jesus and the Apostles is almost complete, although a second work, representing the kidnapping of Elijah, has fared less well. A niche on the right of the chapel contains a stone coffin that tradition assigns to Galla Placidia, the daughter of the Emperor Theodosius who died in 450AD and who is said to have erected the chapel. The left niche holds a second stone coffin, that of the German martyr and Sant'

152

Aquilino himself. The remains of the saint are kept in a crystal and silver urn in a niche of the High Altar.

The staircase by the chapel leads underneath it and was only explored for the first time in 1910. The exploration revealed debris from Roman buildings brought in, it is assumed, to assist with work on the chapel foundations.

Behind the High Altar is the chapel of Sant' Ippolito in which there are beautiful columns of African marble with Corinthian capitals. But for all the magnificence inside, it is for me, the view from across the parkland on the far side of the basilica from the Colonna that holds the eye. That view really is exquisite.

Back to the Duomo Across the parkland make for Via Cardinale Caprera which leads into the tiny Piazza Quasimodo. Here I will recommend a bar and point you in the direction of Johnny Bar, with its brass work and general cleanliness. While you enjoy a break and a coffee you could perhaps contemplate the name of the square. It was not named for the hero (?) of *The Hunchback of Notre Dame* but for the poet Salvatore Quasimodo who lived between 1901 and 1968.

Leave the square along Via Olmetto, then turning into Via Corniggia and follow it around its leftward elbow to Via Amedei. There you will find the Palazzo Recalcati, an elegant sixteenth-century *palazzo* that was much enlarged in the centuries that followed its construction for a well-established Milanese family. The façade was originally brilliantly-coloured brickwork and must have looked better than the current finish of yellow ochre. The graceful wrought-iron balcony is delightful.

In Via Amedei is the Collina Pistoiese, claimed by many to be the best Tuscan restaurant in town; reinforce the heresy and eat Tuscan again. Try the *pasta e fagioli* if you want to do the place justice.

Now go up Via Amedei and then left into a narrow side road, a piece of old Milan, that leads back to the Via Olmetto and Palazzo Brivio. The *palazzo* is interesting for having been painstakingly reconstructed after World War II during which it was badly damaged. The design dates from the fifteenth-century.

From the *palazzo* follow Via Olmetto back into Piazza Sant' Alessandro and return by way of the outward journey back to the Duomo.

Piazza Duomo at night

Sant' Ambrogio and Santa Maria Delle Grazie

Go out of Piazza del Duomo along Via Torino. Take the right-hand side of the road, reaching the church of San Sebastian after passing the entrance to Santa Maria presso San Satiro on the other side.

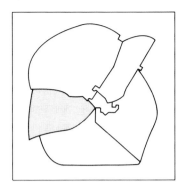

San Sebastiano and San Giorgio

San Sebastiano is Milan's civic church, maintained by money from the City Fathers and used for municipal services. Most notable of these is that on 20 January when dignitaries light candles for the safety of both the city and the church. The church was built in 1577 and is chiefly noticeable for its magnificent Apollo-spacecraft-like top, finished off with a rain-stained copper cupola. Inside, the church is circular: look for the beautiful bronze door of Giacomo Manzù finished in 1951 and the tapestry depicting the martyrdom of St Sebastian. This tapestry is dated to the sixteenth-century, although it is of unknown origin. The tapestry is in the first chapel to the left, the first chapel to the right having a portrait of Sant' Eligio, the patron saint of silver- and goldsmiths. Each year on 25 June the local smiths gather here to give thanks and to offer an example of their work.

To the right shortly you will see Via Valpetrosa. A little way up this street is the Casa dei Grifi, the house of the Grifi, a powerful family at the court of the Sforzas. The house is simple and unprepossessing, but hides a superb Renaissance courtyard.

Luini Fresco, Capella di SS Sacramento, church of San Giorgio

Sant'Ambrogio & Santa Maria delle Grazie

80. S. Maria delle Grazie
81. Casa degli Atellani
82. Basilica of S. Vittore al Corpo
83. Museum of Science and Technology
84. Basilica of S. Ambrogio
85. Pusterla of S. Ambrogio
86. S. Michele sul Dosso
87. S. Bernardino alle Monache
88. S. Sisto
89. Palazzo Stampa Soncino Casati
90. Palazzo of Prospero Visconti
91. S. Giorgio al Palazzo
92. Casa dei Grifi
93. S. Sebastiano
94. Palazzo dei Castani
94a. Leonardo's *Last Supper*

95. S. Sepolcro
95a. Temple of Victory
96. Palazzo Ambrosiana
96a. Castello Cova
97. Palazzo delle Borse
98. S. Maria alla Porta
99. Palazzo Borromeo
100. S. Maria Podone
101. Torre dei Morigi
102. Remains of Roman Circus
103. Remains of Roman Baths
104. Torre dei Gorani
105. Archaeology Museum
106. S. Maurizio
107. Casa Medicea
108. S. Nicolao
109. Palazzo Litta.

Next on the right is the church of San Giorgio al Palazzo. Originally built in 750 on the site of the Imperial Roman palace (which explains the name, *al Palazzo*), this church was rebuilt in the twelfth-century in Romanesque style. It has been restyled several times since, most noticeably when it was given a new, two-level, façade in the eighteenth-century, finished off by a pair of oddly-set obelisks. The façade is backed by a small, but tall, dome and slender campanile, and pierced by three huge doors beyond which the English visitor can hunt for a marble relief of St George killing the dragon from horseback. The main reason why you should visit San Giorgio is to see the magnificent cycle painting of scenes from the Passion of Christ which was completed in 1515 by Bernardino Luini. The series of frescoed panels is in the Capella di ss Sacramento, known in some writings on the church as the Corpus Domini, and is extraordinary. If the caretaker is in the church be sure to ask for the lights to be lit, because, although there are visitor-operable lights to illuminate the lower panels, the lights for the upper panels are controlled from a private room. When the lights are on, do not stand too close to the chapel to view the upper arch panels. Luini was a clever as well as a superb artist, and those panels have been arranged with an eye to perspective; they need to be viewed from the edge of the nave seating. The churches of Italy are renowned for their frescoes, and many in Milan have very fine examples. If you have limited time, or just an interest in, (rather than a passion for) frescoes, content yourself with a visit to the Leonardo beside Santa Maria delle Grazie (*see* page 174) the old church of San Maurizio, if you are lucky enough to find it open, and this Luini Passion series.

Palazzo Stampa-Soncino-Casati Beyond San Giorgio, on the other side of Via Torino, is Palazzo Stampa-Soncino-Casati. You might think that it couldn't be as big as its name, but it is both huge and impressive. It was built in the early 1500s by Massimiliano Stampa, a friend of the last Duke of Milan before the arrival of the governors of Charles V of Spain. He was given important responsibilities under the new regime, which conferred upon him the title of Count of Soncino, and in a very short time the *palazzo* became one of the centres of fashionable city life. The final addition to the name came in the nineteenth-century when the façade was altered by the new owners, the Casati family, the alterations being in Neo-Classical style. This round of improvements involved the making of a new entrance into what is now Via Soncino. The breakthrough into this street required the demolition of several existing houses; history does not record the reaction of the householders.

The *palazzo's* tower dates from the original sixteenth-century work and is named the Torre dei Soncino; it also has an alternative name, Torre dell'Imperatore, the Emperor being Charles V. The two pillars at the tower's top support a globe, a two-headed eagle, a crown and cross. The collection symbolizes the Emperor, the eagle, crown and cross being straightforward; the two pillars represent the Pillars of Hercules – believed to be the Straits of Gibraltar in Greek mythology through which the Emperor came in order to conquer the globe. History suggests that the Emperor was much impressed.

Inside, the *palazzo* is elegantly courtyarded, the yard created by porticoed galleries on three levels.

Beyond the *palazzo* is the square known locally as Il Carrobbio, although the official name is Largo Carrobbio. The square derives its name from the Latin *quadrivium*, a crossroads, the old Roman city gate lying near here. The road through the gate – *the Ticinum* – led to Pavia, and the gate then (as now) was called the Ticinese.

On the right side of Il Carrobbio as you enter is the church of San Sisto. Legend has it that this church was founded in 770 by Desiderio, king of the Lombards, although it was rebuilt in the early seventeenth-century. During World War I the church was deconsecrated and used as a military store. Following the war the building fell into disrepair, but it has been partially restored by Francesco Messina, a sculptor of the Realist school, who uses it as a studio. Messina is a very well-known Italian Sculptor whose work is seen throughout the country; a visit here will give you a good idea of what is now considered to be at the forefront of Italian art. There is a collection of Messina sculptures as well as drawings and prints. The bronzes, especially, are beautiful and Messina shows a particularly delicate touch when making a nude study.

Via Lanzone Leave Il Carrobbio along Via del Torchio, on the far side of the square from San Sisto, and follow this away from the city centre. The road becomes the Via Lanzone and here, to the right, is Via Circo in which stands the Brasera Meneghina (at No. 10) a very good Milanese restaurant you should visit as a penance for eating at those Tuscan restaurants. The Brasera is closed on Fridays, so go another day to take advantage of the garden and the risotto. If it is chilly they light a fire in the old fireplace.

Where Via Lanzone starts, immediately to the right is the Palazzo di Prospero Visconti, a huge but hardly handsome building completed in 1591 by Prospero Visconti. It was severely damaged during World War II, after which it was largely rebuilt. Architecturally, the *palazzo* is said to stand at the dividing line between the Renaissance and Lombard Baroque schools, but it is chiefly famous for having perhaps been lived in by another member of the Visconti family, Bernardino, made famous as L'Innominato by the writer Manzoni. Look for the snake symbol of the Visconti family.

Further on, to the left, is the church of San Bernardino alle Monache. This church has an odd history, having been built, rebuilt, re-rebuilt, deconsecrated and reconsecrated. Despite all this it is of little interest, except for the quality of the brickwork and the delightful campanile.

Follow Via Lanzone as it bends to the right. In December the fair (*see* page 167) extends right along this road. To the right, about halfway along there is a fine Baroque church dedicated to Sant' Agostino. The site is said to have been the one where the saint was baptised by Sant' Ambrogio. Despite this story being repeated as true on the facade of the church it is not so.

At the end, just as you exit the gloomy, high-wall-enclosed road for the light of the square, look to the left for a view of the church of San Michele sul Dusso. The church is so called because it was built under the original town wall – *sul Dosso*, 'below the rise'. It is of very ancient origin, although what you see today is early sixteenth-century. The campanile is very graceful.

Beside the church is the Pusterla of Sant' Ambrogio, all that now remains of the dozen or so *pusterla* or minor doors which stood in the old town wall between the six great doors. On a fine morning in May 1385, Gian Galeazzo Visconti, passing through Milan, asked his uncle Bernabò, then governor of the city, to meet him at this gate. Bernabò came, quickly and unarmed expecting

The Pusterla, Sant' Ambrogio

the meeting to be a joyous one. When he arrived he greeted his nephew, but Gian Galeazzo gave orders to his own men to capture his uncle, to chain him and to throw him into prison.

Of the two towers only one – the one on the right – is believed to be wholly original. The left tower holds a collection of antique arms, including rare weapons such as Napoleonic shotguns. There are helmets covering the period from the Etruscan, a fine bronze, to that of the *condottiero* Gabrio Serbelloni. There is a Colt pistol that once belonged to Garibaldi and a fine collection of swords.

Basilica of Sant' Ambrogio The Basilica of Sant' Ambrogio is second only to the Duomo in importance as a religious building in the city.

The story goes that Ambrose (Ambrogio) was born in Gaul the son of a Roman prefect and was intended for a life in law after studying in Rome. He was sent to Milan as governor of the region, arriving soon after the city's bishop had died. As was the norm, the people were electing a new bishop and so divided were opinions that there was a general uproar which Ambrose

Just before entering the magnificent courtyard that stands at the front of the Basilica of Sant'Ambrogio, look for the stone column at the corner of the church. This is a Roman column with a Corinthian capital, a last remnant of the Imperial Palace, but there is a nice legend associated with the curious pair of holes at the column's base. The legend has it that the devil himself came to Milan to try to tempt Sant' Ambrogio in order to prevent him from building his church. The good man would not listen to him, and growing exasperated with his continuing attempts, grabbed hold of him and threw him out. The devil collided with the column and the holes are where his horns stuck into the stone. As a result the column is known as the Colonna del Diavolo.

160

attempted to calm. He spoke to the feuding crowd, talking of the need for peace and harmony. They were so moved that they decided Ambrose was the man they wanted for their bishop. Ambrose, who does not appear even to have been a Christian at the time, was reluctant, but an appeal by the city to the Emperor received an enthusiastic response and Ambrose was persuaded. He was baptised, hurriedly taught the Holy Rites and installed as bishop on 7 December 374. About five years later he started to build the church that now bears his name.

As a site he chose an old cemetery outside one of the city gates, an area where early Christian martyrs had been burned for their faith. There was probably already a church of some sort here, dedicated to St Vittorio, one of the martyrs.

It was Ambrogio's early wish to be buried in the church, beside the bodies of two martyrs, St Gervaso and St Protaso, beneath a *ciborium*, a canopy raised on columns, near the altar. When he died, on 5 April 397, he was laid to rest as he had wished, and the church was renamed in his honour.

In the last years of the eighth-century work began on the building of a Benedictine monastery on the site of what is now the Catholic University. As well as building their monastery, the monks also remodelled the original church of Sant' Ambrogio; their alterations were in prototype Lombard Romanesque, but they all but obliterated the earlier building. Only a part of the walls and the bases of some columns remain, although two inlaid panels in glass and marble survived and can be seen in the museum. The complete reworking of the site took many years and included, in the late ninth-century, the exhumation of the bodies of the three saints whose remains were placed in a sepulchre that had, it is believed, been used for the Emperor Valentian II. The Archbishop who undertook the exhumation, Angilberto II, also commissioned the artist Volvinio to create a golden altar. This altar is still in the church, and is one of the great masterpieces of ninth-century goldsmithing. The altar is panelled, the panels depicting scenes from the life of Sant' Ambrogio. The work is almost beyond description and on no account should be missed. The verses on the altar explain why the Archbishop felt the need to carry out the work. In simple terms, he was driven by the need to pay homage to the founding saint.

Devil's Column, Sant' Ambrogio

**Entrance courtyard, Sant'
Ambrogio**

The monastery beside the church became one of the most significant in Europe, reaching the height of its importance at the time of the Sforzas. Later, by edict of Pope Paul II, the Benedictine monks were replaced by Cistercians from the nearby Abbey of Chiaravalle. An expansion of the buildings took place; Bramante was brought in to add a canonica but he stopped work when his patron, Ludovico il Moro, fell from power, having added only the door through which the visitor enters the church. Work did not start again in earnest until Federico Borromeo finally commissioned Francesco Maria Richini in 1630.

Finally, the bodies of the saints were moved again, being placed in a silver and crystal cabinet in 1897, the fifteen-hundredth anniversary of the death of Sant' Ambrogio.

The atrium, or entrance hall, of the basilica is arcaded on three sides, the fourth forming part of the façade of the church, a Romanesque triangle, but with large, deeply-cut niches. To the right of the church is the ninth-century monk's bell tower (*Campanile dei Monaci*) while to the left is that of the canons of the church (*Campanile dei Canonici*). Beneath the arcades are various sections of the older buildings found during rebuilding work.

In the atrium façade are three doors, the middle one of which has panels with scenes from the lives of David and Saul. Inside the basilica there are so many treasures that it is difficult to know what to exclude so that this book does not become a catalogue for the church. Do see the early Christian sarcophagus, said to be of Stilicone, but more likely that of the Emperor Graziano who died in 383. It is finely carved with scenes from the Old and the New Testament.

The golden altar of Volvinio is the next treasure, and an interpretation of its panels does help the visitor to savour the work. The altar is a large wooden box without a cover, faced with a gold and silver laminate, finely worked and encrusted with jewels, pearls and cameos. The front panel has a Latin cross at the centre, with Christ in the centre and evangelists in the arms. In the corners are the twelve apostles. The six panels on the left represent the Annunciation, the nativity, the presentation at the temple, the miracle of Carna, the calling of Matthew and the Transfiguration. In the six panels on the right are Jesus ordering the merchants from the temple, Jesus curing the blind, the

**Volvinio's Altar, Sant'
Ambrogio**

**The Tomb of The Saints, Sant'
Ambrogio**

Crucifixion, the descent of the Holy Spirit, the Resurrection and the Ascension.

The left side of the altar has in its centre a jewelled cross with the saints Naborre, Martino, Nazaro and Materno at the ends of its arms and angels and cherubim filling the spaces around. The right side of the altar is the same as the left, but here the saints are Ambrogio, Protaso, Gervaso and Simpliciano. The rear of the altar, facing the choir, has scenes from the life of Sant' Ambrogio in the edge panels, with the Archangels Michael and Gabriel at the centre, below which are Ambrogio crowning Volvinio and Archbishop Angilberto presenting the saint with a model of the church. This rear panel to the altar is in silver, is widely believed to be the best part of the altar and is the only section to have been completed personally by Volvinio.

In the centre of the choir, against the wall, is the marble bishop's throne dating from the ninth-century; its stone seat is the one on which Sant' Ambrogio sat in the fourth-century. In times gone by pregnant Milanese women would come to sit on the throne as this was supposed to bring a less painful labour. To the sides of the throne are magnificent choir stalls dating from the fifteenth-century with carved backs of stylized trees and animals

The votive chapel of San Vittore, reached from the seventh chapel of the nave on the right, was built originally in the fourth-century to hold the remains of the saint, the remains of San Satiro, the brother of Ambrogio, being added at a later time. The chapel is believed to stand at the area of the original cemetery where the bodies of the martyrs were interred. The chapel is square and has a beautiful cupola with a splendid fifteenth-century mosaic showing a crowned St Victor holding a book with his name inscribed on it. There is also a fresco of Sant' Ambrogio, the oldest-known image of the saint. In the crypt beneath the chapel is a late Imperial sarcophagus containing the relics of San Vittorio and San Satiro.

The crypt that holds the bodies of the three saints lies below the choir. It is not always open, and when it is the queue to enter it can be long and agitated. Access is restricted, however, with batches of visitors being counted in and no new people allowed in until that batch has progressed around that cabinet and made its way out at the far side. Those who are patient, or who are lucky enough to be alone – I once visited the basilica midweek and midmorning and was the only person in the crypt – are guaranteed a sight of the remains. The crypt and cabinet are remarkably ornate, but the sight of the saints itself can be a shock. The bodies are laid out in fine vestments and are not well preserved – except in the relative sense. For visitors not used to seeing saints (or any other bodies for that matter), coming face to face with bemitred semi-skulls is quite an experience. The crypt is not, perhaps, for the overly sensitive, but although a little macabre, it is not grisly and must be recommended to anyone who is lucky enough to be in Milan when the crypt is open.

The visitor can leave the church from a door at the far end from the courtyard entrance, and this exit allows direct access to the Museum of Sant' Ambrogio. The museum is sited above Bramante's rectory, reached from the canonica of the same architect, a beautiful arcaded walkway, and holds many sacred items from the history of the basilica. There are fine vestments, including a fourth-century Oriental damask decorated with hunting scenes, and mosaics, including the marble and tile panels from the original church of Sant' Ambrogio. One, almost devoid of tiles now, shows the lamb that, even in the fourth-century, was a mystical Christian symbol. There are fragments of the door of the first church, and a section of what is said to be Sant' Ambrogio's bed. There is a collection of ancient parchments, some tapestries and altar covers and a few paintings. These include a Zenale triptych and a Luini fresco.

The museum entrance is from the ambulatory that runs around two sides of a semi-courtyard to the west of the church. Visible from this court is the Temple of Victory. The temple, set close to but outside the Sant' Ambrogio complex, was built in 1928 in honour of the men of Milan who fell in World War I. It is an imposing structure, not least because its white marble is in such stark contrast to the warm red-browns of Sant' Ambrogio. At the top is a revolving lighthouse.

Leaving the courtyard along the side of the temple brings the visitor to Piazza Sant' Ambrogio. This is the site of the ancient Poliandro, the Holy Area, which in the second century AD held the tombs of the first Milanese Christian martyrs and saints. Not surprisingly, it was here that Sant' Ambrogio erected his church, the church taking the name of its founder when he had chosen to be buried in it. Before the Christian era the piazza was the site of an Imperial Palace and in the Middle Ages it became the centre for religious processions. In the weeks before Christmas the fair known as Oh Bei, Oh Bei (from the calls of the stallholders) would be held in the square, and this tradition still continues, with stalls not only in the square itself, but also in many of the adjoining alleys.

To the right as you exit from the Sant' Ambrogio courtyard is the Catholic University of the Sacred Heart which has, since 1932, occupied the old monastery of Sant' Ambrogio. The old building has remained intact, although there have been several additions, most particularly the façade where the statue of Christ the King by Castiglioni has been added.

The old monastery was to have had four cloisters, but only two were completed. Both survive, one Doric, the other Ionic, and each is now filled with noisy students rather than contemplative monks. You should join the students for a view of **The Catholic University**

Castello Cova

the fine, tree-filled cloisters. The site is not quite as good as that of Ca'Grande, being more enclosed and less spacious, but for all that it must be a very fine place to study.

San Vittore Al Corpo If you walk through the university you will come out close to the entrance to the Basilica. From there, go across the lower square and leave it to reach Via Giosuè Carducci at its junction with Via San Vittore. On the corner the castle from the Disney film set is Castello Cova built in 1910. Go past this and on down Via San Vittore to reach the Basilica of San Vittore al Corpo and Milan's Museum of Science and Technology.

The basilica has a very long history, the first having been built in the fourth-century on the site of a cemetery next to an Imperial Mausoleum. This position led to the first church having *ad corpus* attached to its name. This was retained when the present, eighth-century church was dedicated to the martyr San Vittore. In the eleventh-century the church was given to a nearby Benedictine monastery, and the monks rebuilt it in Romanesque style. Later still the church was completely remodelled and the chapel of St Gregory, actually the remnant of the Roman mausoleum, was demolished. This last refurbishment was in the hands of Alessi to whom we owe the façade. Inside, the church is surprisingly large, the nave vaulting being elaborately decorated. The wood carving of the choir stalls is sixteenth-century and very good.

The part of Milan near the basilica was still a suburb when, at the end of the fifteenth-century, Ludovico Il Moro made a gift to Leonardo of a magnificent vineyard halfway between the convent of San Vittore al Corpo and the church of Santa Marie delle Grazie (then being refurbished under the guidance of Donato Bramante). The site was very suitable for Leonardo as he was at the time working on his famous fresco, but he had to leave his pleasant house, a fact that greatly displeased him. One story has him moving here to a building that was once a monastery attached to the church of San Vittore, and is now a museum dedicated to him.

The museum houses one gallery that is dedicated to the great man, a 120-metre-long gallery past a glass panel delicately and subtly engraved with a portrait of him. The gallery has exhibits and working models of some of Leonard's greatest achievements in various fields – aeronautics, engineering and anatomy.

Altogether, the gallery is one of the finest tributes to an individual that it is possible to imagine.

Elsewhere in the building and the annexes that stand in the grounds of the old monastery the collections are impressive. There is a shed full of railway engines, a yard and a building full of planes; there are cars – some cut in half to show construction and workings, motorbikes and ships, as well as specific exhibitions on metallurgy, electricity, electronics, astronomy and so on. The section of the museum that is given over to hands-on experiments for children is terrific. With all such collections it is difficult to pick favourites; indeed, should you? Just to offer food for thought and comment, the equipment of Umberto Nobile on his expedition to the North Pole is extraordinary for its apparent lack of sophistication, and the *Ebe*, the Italian naval training ship, is beautiful. Finding a full-rigged sailing ship in a museum is astonishing. I also liked the case of violin parts that showed the constructional method for the instrument. The Umberto Nobile equipment is actually part of another museum, the Naval Educational Museum, which shares the site with the bigger Science and Technology Museum, and is equally worthwhile.

Santa Maria delle Grazie From the museum and church continue along Via San Vittore to it junction with Via Zenale and go right along that to reach the church of Santa Maria delle Grazie, one of the great highlights of a trip to Milan.

Before reaching the church you will pass, at Nos. 65 and 67, the Casa degli Atellani, the House of the Atellani, a pair of Renaissance houses – although there has been considerable renovation work in the twentieth-century – which belonged to the two equerries of Ludovico il Moro. Each of the houses maintains its original courtyard. Legend has it that Leonardo stayed at one of the houses when he was painting the *Last Supper*.

Across the road is both the church and the building that houses the *Last Supper*.

In 1463 Guiniforte Solari gave the Dominican Order land in the part of the city close to the castle where he served as Commander of the Sforza army. The order decided to build a convent and Guiniforte Solari was employed to design both the convent and a church to stand beside .it. This church – to Santa

Leonardo's Hall, Museum of Science of Technology

One of the exhibits, Museum of Science of Technology

Marie delle Grazie, St Mary of the Favours, was in Lombard Gothic style, but was changed dramatically when, in 1942, Ludovico il Moro decided to remodel it. The great architect Donato Bramante was given the work and he began by pulling down much of the earlier work, elongating what remained and adding a new cloister and sacristy. Ludovico decided that both he and his wife, Beatrice d'Este, should be buried in the church and when she died Beatrice was indeed interred. However, when his death came, local police prevented Ludovico from joining his wife. Politics also prevented the monumental effigies, that Solari had completed from being erected in the church. The effigies, delicate works in polished marble, can be seen today in the Certosa of Pavia.

Today what we see lies behind Solari's façade, a beautiful work in brick with a triangle of circular windows *(oculi)*, a surprising and delightful feature, above a row of slender, arched windows. At the centre of the façade is a larger circular window. Along the right side, the very long right side, of the church the interplay of slender, arched and circular windows is repeated. Then, at the far end, comes the apse of Bramante. It is difficult to believe that this is not the man's masterpiece, as the whole structure looks to be perfect, not one column too many or too few, not one wrong colour change in the building medium. The apse is so beautiful that is has to be seen to be appreciated. Do come here.

The church of Santa Marie delle Grazie

Inside, the church's three naves are divided by arches supported by columns that lead on to superb cross vaults that are delicately frescoed. The majesty of the construction is beyond words. At the end of the long naves is the inner side of Bramante's apse supported on four massive arches. The medallions here, of Evangelists, are attributed to Amadeo. In the chapel of the Madonna delle Grazie – the oratory of the first church, and the chapel that gave the church its name – there is superb stucco work.

There are two cloisters. The convent cloister, the largest of the two that survive, is known as the Cloister of the Dead and is the work of Solari. It is a good work, but cannot compare with the small cloister, sometimes known as the Cloister of the Frogs, that Bramante added when he remodelled the church. The name

Bramante's Apse from the Cloister of the Frogs, Santa Marie delle Grazie

doubtless derives from the pond at the centre of the small cloister garden. Around the edge, the walkway is covered, and separated from the garden by a low wall and open arcade. From the cloister the view to Bramante's apse is wonderful, the full glory of the building rising above the delicate garden; the whole scene, especially the different colours of the stone and brickwork, is enhanced by the interplay of light and dark, sunlight and shadow, among the arcades.

Leonardo's Fresco In 1495 Ludovico il Moro commissioned Leonardo da Vinci to paint the end wall of the refectory of the convent of Santa Maria delle Grazie. Leonardo decided to illustrate the Last Supper, and drawings now held at Windsor Castle in England suggest that he wished to capture the moment when Jesus told the Disciples that one of them would betray him. Judas, fourth from the left, is represented grasping a small bag of money. Leonardo decided to use an unusual technique for the fresco, *tempera forte* rather than *buon forte*. The latter, the more normal method, required painting on to wet plaster so that the work, dried in to the wall covering. The advantage of the method is that the painting is very well protected against the rigours of time. The disadvantage is that the work needs to be completed very quickly. The technique is also not very tolerant of errors. Leonardo chose a technique that would allow him time to develop the work, and also to re-touch if necessary, but the technique was not well understood in terms of its ageing.

The artist set up scaffolding against the wall from which he could work and painted on and off for two years. History records that on some days he would paint for just a few minutes, on some he would work without stopping for hours, while on others he would not turn up at all. In short, he behaved just as a genius should.

Twenty years after the fresco was completed Antonio de Beatis arrived in Milan to view it. He found it very excellent, although beginning to be spoiled, owing to either the dampness of the wall or to some other accident. De Beatis was correct in his first guess. The painting technique allowed flakes of paint to curl away from the wall. Condensation then got behind the paint layer and attacked the underlying plaster sizing. This lifted or, worse, became infected with airborne moulds which discoloured the paint and caused it to flake even more. Fifty years after the visit of de Beatis the situation was so bad that restoration work was needed, and in the three and a half centuries that have followed this restoration work has continued. Today the visitor views the painting over the heads of the academic restorers. As if the painting had not enough to bear with the effects of age and moisture-induced deterioration, the refectory building was almost completely destroyed by the Allied bombings of 1943. Miraculously, some would say (and it is difficult not to believe in miracles), the painting survived the raid intact.

Of the painting itself it is difficult to form an objective opinion. This is due in part to the lighting in the room, subdued so as to avoid further damage to the work, in part to the fact that the visitor is kept well back so that expelled breath does not cause too much of the condensation that is the major destructive agent, and in part to the fact that the visitor has been told in advance that he is viewing a masterpiece by Leonardo. To avoid disappointment, see if you can obtain a copy of a book on the painting so that you can study the elements of the work before going to see it. The detail in the hands of the figures, in the folds of their clothing and in their faces is remarkable.

And finally, before you leave the refectory, do spend time in front of the crucifixion of Donato di Montorfano. Most give little more than a passing glance to this fine work, in its way another masterpiece. That is sad, for it is more accessible − in both senses of the word − than the Leonardo, and well worth some of your time.

Corso Magenta After the church and painting, go along Corso Magenta towards the centre of the city. There is much of interest in this road, and it starts with the ruins of the Casa Medicea at No. 29. These comprise the remains of a brown stone wall in the courtyard of a ruined building − all that has survived of the Milanese house of Lorenzo de Medici − which was given to him by the Sforzas.

Opposite the ruin, a little way up and to the right in Via San Nicolao, is the church of the saint. It has not had a fortunate history, being close enough to the castle to have been in danger every time the city changed hands, which was often after the church's construction in 1659. Eventually the church was deconsecrated and used to store hay and wood, only being reconsecrated in the latter half of the nineteenth-century. At that time it was restored, but this restoration was not too successful.

Palazza Litta The next building of interest is Palazzo Litta. The *palazzo* – also called Palazzo Arese on occasions – it is the work of Francesco Maria Richini, who built it for Count Bartolomeo Arese, although the impressive façade is a century newer, the work of Bolla in the mid-eighteenth-century. At the same time the interior was remodelled, a huge pincer-like staircase being added. This feature took away the breath of all who saw it when the *palazzo* was the venue for a Milan society party. Overall, it is now agreed that Palazzo Litta is the finest Lombard house of its period. Although it is occasionally called after its first owner, the

Palazzo Litta

palazzo is more usually associated with the Marquis Litta, who used it, in part, as a gallery and library, the latter holding one of the most important sets of plans of major sacred buildings in existence.

However, although the collection was important, it was the parties that held the attention. These were legendary in Milan, particularly when held under the direction of Maria Theresa of Austria and Eugenio Beauharnais, the Viceroy of Milan at the time of Napoleon. Later, during the Five Days in 1848, the story is told that the Marquess Litta went to Marshall Radetzky the infamous Austrian commander, who held the castle, and asked that he should spare her and the *palazzo* if he should shell the city. The Marshall is said to have told her that her entreaties would fail as he was completely insensitive to women and their wiles. This somewhat surprised the Marquess, and indeed the whole of Milan, as the Marshall had, at the time, a Milanese mistress who had borne him four children – despite his being in his mid-seventies – in addition to a legitimate wife who had given him five more.

The *palazzo* is Milan's finest staircase, a sumptuous design that is in contrast to the simplicity of much of the rest. These is a suite of rooms that is decorated in the style of Louis XV and another room hung with old and precious silks.

Detail of the facade, Palazzo Litta

Archaeological Museum Across the road from the *palazzo* is Milan's Archaeological Museum. Its housing, in two remaining cloisters of the Monastero Maggiore, gives the entrance a richness that matches well its collection of items from ancient Mediolanum. The entrance is in rococo style, with one really exquisite section where a scroll in black marble extols the virtues of the Benedictine House. In the centre of the arcade of granite Doric columns that forms the only complete cloister is a rock from the Val Camonica with carvings that are 3,000 years old. Val Camonica lies north of Lake Iseo, the smallest of the large northern Italian lakes which lie to the east of Milan. In the valley about a quarter of a million such rock engravings have been found, covering a span of time from 8,000 years ago until Roman times. So important is this area that it has been designated a World Heritage Site. Next are a series of Roman finds from the city itself, these being positioned beneath a span of the cloister.

The bells of Monastero Maggiore, Museum of Archaeology

Within the covered section of the museum the finest pieces are, in many ways, a matter of personal choice, but do be sure to see the torso of Hercules, found in the city in 1827. The torso turned up during excavations at the church of San Vito al Pasquirolo on the site of what is now believed to have been the Roman Herculean baths. The baths date from the Maximian era, that is the fourth-century AD. However, the assumption that the statue and baths are intimately joined is not justified; the statue is almost certainly older than the fourth-century and baths were not named after the god – Christianity was the religion of the day – but after another of Maximian's names. There is no scholarly doubt about the statue being Hercules (in fact, it was probably taken to the baths because of that fact), the pose being the classic Greek one adopted for statues of the god.

Equally fascinating is the Trivulzio cage-cup found at Novara in 1935. This intricate piece of work was carved from a single piece of glass in the fourth-century, and bears the inscription *Bibe Vivas Multis Annis* 'drink, you will live many years.' Elsewhere there is a fine head of Jupiter from the Sforza castle, a silver sacrificial plate from the fourth-century, items from the Bronze Age culture at Golasecca and from a sixth-century BC soldier's tomb uncovered at Sesto Calende. There are also items from the Etruscan, Greek and Egyptian worlds.

The enclosed section of the museum gives way to a second cloister that formerly stood at the back of the old convent. Here there are two towers of great interest. The first, Torre Quadrata del Monastero Maggiore, is Roman in its lower reaches, although the main section is Lombardian Pre-Romanesque. The convent used it as a campanile. The other tower, the Torre di Massimiano, is Roman, built in the third-century AD. Anciently it formed a corner tower in the Roman town wall, which explains its heavy construction. It does not of itself explain its shape: the tower is twenty-four-sided which is intriguing.

San Maurizio Next door to the museum is San Maurizio, an excellent Renaissance church built between the two sets of cloisters of an old Benedictine nunnery, the Monastero Maggiore. This was founded, it is believed, by Theodolinda, wife of the Lombard king Desiderius, at the start of the seventh-century. The house was called 'Maggiore' because it was the biggest and the most important in the city. It was also rich: within its walls there were gardens and orchards, and the abbess frequently wore a diadem and walked around the city with an escorting band of archers. The name was changed to San Maurizio in 914 when Otto I gave the convent a phial containing blood of the saint.

The nunnery was closed in 1798, and part of the older buildings were demolished in 1863 to make way for the Via Luini. This is an ironic choice of name, the church being famous for its frescoes by Bernardino Luini who painted them under the patronage of Alessandro Bentivoglio, governor of the city, whose daughter, Bianca, had become a nun at the convent.

The two remaining cloisters of the nunnery now house the Archeological museum.

From the outside the multi-storeyed church is deceptively simple, apart perhaps from the circular window in the third storey.

On the other side of Via Luini is the campanile of the old nunnery, the Torre Quadrata, or square tower. In its lower section this campanile is believed to have been part of an old prison but the upper section is Lombard Pre-Romanesque, probably from the eighth-century and was incorporated into the nunnery as a bell tower.

Luini Fresco, church of San Maurizio

Inside, the church is still divided as it was when one half was for the exclusive use of the nuns. The church is wonderfully lit, the ceiling vault having circular windows that throw interacting rivers of light into the building. The medallions on the nave arches, each of which shows the face of a saint, are attributed to Antonio Boltraffio, but it is the frescoes you have come to see. Of these the most important are in the third chapel on the right, the last work by Bernardino Luini before his death in 1532, showing scenes from the martyrdom of St Catherine of Alexandria. It is said that the face of St Catherine is that of the Countess of Challant, who was beheaded in Milan in 1526 for having incited her lover into murdering someone who had made disparaging remarks about her.

Bernardino Luini also painted the chapel's partition wall – apart from the Adoration of the Magi which is the work of Antonio Campi – including himself, the man with the white beard, in his work of Alessandro Bentivoglio and the saints.

On the opposite side of the church is more work by Luini, including the martyrdom of San Maurizio and the saint being offered a model of the new church. The fourth chapel on the left includes a copy of Leonardo's *Last Supper*, possible by a son of Luini.

Through an opening on the left side of the altar the back room of the church is reached, dark and low and filled with fine, but very dark, carved stalls. This room has great presence. It also has some quite surprising frescoes by Bernardino Luini, who shows himself to be a landscape artist of great delicacy and touch. His series of pastoral works in the alcoves of the left wall are impressive.

All visitors to Milan should try to see San Maurizio, if they want to understand Italian frescoed sacred painting.

Milan's Towers Those with an interest in the Roman history of the city should now go down Via Bernardino Luini to reach the second turning on the left, Via Vigna. There, at No.1, a high and massive brick wall is all that remains of the Roman Circus. The lower section of the wall is a mixture of mortar and river stones, while the upper part, of large bricks, shows some evidence of later, possibly Medieval patching. The Circus itself, built by Traiano in the second-century AD, was the most impressive building in Imperial Milan. It was used for horse-racing, and was about 500 metres long and 85 metres wide. another section of it, part of the curved foundation, can be seen in a side wall of No.7 Via Circo.

Even if you are not planning to go to Via Vigna it is worthwhile to go down Via Luini as far as Via Ansperto, the first road to the left, in order to obtain the best view of the Torre dei Gorani.

Towards the end of the twelfth-century, in the disputes over who was to have control of the free cities of northern Italy, the nobles or the communes, many of the nobles started to build towers. The reasons are twofold. Firstly, the towers offered security in the event that the power struggle took a turn for the worse and the noble needed a secure bolt-hole; secondly, the towers represented power, and meant that the owner was not to be trifled with. In later years the nobles had passages connecting their *palazzos* with the towers; some were secret and underground, some above ground but were at first-floor or higher level so that the passage users were protected. The towers had by then also become a real statue symbol, with power etiquette decreeing how high a tower could be. There were also odd rules – no tower could be inherited by a girl, and boys were 'initiated' into the tower at the age of manhood, about 15 at the time. Although Milan can no longer boast the number and quality of

Torre dei Gorani

towers that San Gimignano in Tuscany can – indeed, if it ever could boast a similar collection – it does have a couple of nice examples.

The Torre dei Gorani is often claimed to be the sole survivor of Milan's 100 towers, but close by is another that gives the lie to this. The Gorani Tower defended the house of the Gorani in the fourteenth-century, and is brick built and finished with windows that have columns of contrasting Angera stone. The tower finished with a overhung tiled roof that could justifiably be called 'cute', but its position, behind corrugated iron in a dog-patrolled site, is hardly a showcase. In fact, the site holds the remains of the Roman Baths, and the circular plan of the three parts of a typical baths – the *frigidarium, tepidarium* and *calidarium* – is visible. This building too was of mortar and river stones. The presence of these remains makes the neglect even more tragic.

The other tower close to the Gorani, the Torre dei Morigi, is reached by going right, down Via Brisa, at the end of Via Ansperto. This survivor from the fourteenth-century was shortened in the seventeenth-century. There was an earlier tower on the same site, and Lanzone da Corte was locked up in it in 1047 by his fellow nobles for having defended the common city dwellers. He was tortured so shamefully that, says a local historian, 'I do not wish to continue with the story.' In fact, the nobles are said to have decreed that da Corte, who 'wrapped himself in the dung of the people should be made to eat the dung'. And that is what he was apparently forced to do for the last few days before he was executed.

In the later tower Bernabo Visconti installed his favourite consort, Giovannola Montebretto, so that she would be secure from others who might seek her favours.

Back in Corso Magenta you reach Via Santa Maria alla Porta in which stands the church of the same name. It was the last work of Francesco Maria Richini who completed it in 1652 building on the site of an earlier church. The name derives from that earlier church which stood beside one of the Roman city gates. An octagonal chapel that once stood beside the church and housed a miraculous portrait of the Virgin was destroyed by bombing. The only memory of it now is a round window with the frescoed image of the Little Madonna of Miracles, a replica of the original.

Go back briefly to Corso Magenta to see the Palazzo delle Borse. This has an imposing façade but it is chiefly of interest because it incorporates the remains of the Roman theatre which was revealed by excavations as late as 1979. The theatre was built at the time of Augustus. A tracing of the original lines of the walls suggests the theatre could hold about 10,000 people.

Piazza Borromeo At the Y-junction at the end of the

The church of Santa Maria Podone and San Carlo's Statue, Piazza Borromeo

street beyond the church of Santa Maria alla Porta take the right fork, Via Borromeo, and follow it to the square of the same name. To the right as you enter the square is Palazzo Borromeo, the family home – while they were in Milan that is – and at one time the home of San Carlo and his cousin, Cardinal Federico. Externally the building is, frankly, drab; its brickwork is dark, its roof tiles likewise, its window shutters brown, but it does have the one of the best Lombard Gothic doorways (even if this feature looks a little out of place). Look for the camel emblem of the Borromeos that is carved at the apex. Within the *palazzo* there are fine courtyards, one so beautiful, with its pointed arch arcades and decorated façade, that it makes you wonder why the outside of the house could not have been given the same elegant treatment.

In the piazza, between the family *palazzo* and the church of Santa Maria Podone, is a statue of San Carlo Borromeo, a bronze that once stood in the Piazza Cordusio. It was placed there by the saint's cousin Federico to replace a plague altar, but in 1779 the carriage of the Austrian governor of the city, Francesco III, the duke of d'Este, collided with it. The governor insisted that the accident had been the fault of the statue and it was moved to its present position.

The church behind the statue, Santa Maria Podone, although founded in the ninth-century by a Milanese with the nickname 'Podone', owes its present style to the Borromeo family who had made this part of Milan their own by the sixteenth-century. The first modifications were put in hand by Count Vitaliano Borromeo in the fifteenth-century, and Cardinal Federico Borromeo continued the work in the following century.

The façade is pure Baroque with a triangular upper section above a sculpted window, side panels of heavy design and a doorway where the triangular construction is repeated, held up by four huge Corinthian columns. Inside, be sure to see the sculpted relief of the Madonna and Child between two believers, the work of Cristoforo Luvoni in 1483. Also of interest is a painting near the second altar on the left, an enthroned Madonna with Child between two saints, known as the Madonna of the Birth, because expectant Milanese mothers came to pray before it for the safe delivery of their child.

Piazza San Sepolcro and Palazzo dell' Ambrosiana Go through the square and left out of it and right down Via Bollo to reach Piazza San Sepolcro. This is a pretty little piazza only a short distance from the Duomo yet as well sheltered from the noise and bustle of the city as is Piazza dei Mercanti. It represents the centre of the old city of Mediolanum, the crossing-point of the city's two great Roman roads. The Palazzo dei Castani to the right occupies the site of an old city baths. From the piazza the Via Bollo leads to Cinque Vie, five Ways, a famous old alleyway that is little changed since Medieval times.

The Palazzo dei Castini has a fine façade with delicate first-floor balconies of wrought iron and a beautiful Renaissance door between pillars of Angera stone. The doorway holds two medallions of Roman emperors and a motto in Greek wishing everyone good luck.

The first church on the site of San Sepolcro which stands on the other side of the square from the *palazzo* was built in the early eleventh-century, although the shell of what you now see dates from 1100. The name, Holy Sepulchre, derives from the church having been built to the plan of the church of the same name in Jerusalem, the new building being at the expense of a descendant of the first founder, who had just returned from the Crusades. Although the church has been much modified since 1100, the façade has been restored to its original, early Lombard, style. It is well set, between a pair of matching campaniles. The church's crypt – of interesting very early Romanesque design, dating from the earliest church on the site – runs the length of the building and is used for occasional art exhibitions.

Attached to the church is a building that holds a permanent art exhibition that is one of the best in the city.

The Palazzo dell' Ambrosiana is a huge building begun in the seventeenth-century to contain the library and art gallery of Cardinal Federico Borromeo. The building is a little severe, but the art treasures inside more than compensate. From the entrance, in Piazza Pio XI, on the opposite side of the *palazzo* from Piazza San Sepolcro, the visitor can reach the gallery. The gallery works are arranged in approximate chronological order, starting with the fourteenth-century and working through to the nineteenth. Of the earlier works, exhibited in Room 1, there are some virtually priceless examples of painting on wood, one a Botticelli, the Madonna of the Canopy. Elsewhere there are several paintings by

Leonardo's *Musician*, Ambrosiana

Bernardino Luini of which the delicate, informal Infant St John with lamb (in Room 7), and the more formal Holy Family (in Room 8), are worth more than a passing glance. The Leonardo Room (Room 8) contains not only the Luini but the Portrait of a Musician that is now agreed to be a Leonardo by all credible authorities. A second Leonardo, a portrait of, it is believed, Beatrice d'Este, is now thought to be not by the master, but by the Milanese painter Giovanni Ambrogio de Predis. Since not only the artist but also the subject are attributed, the work is something of a mystery. Two rooms contain Flemish and German work, the former with many works by Jan Breughel – most are his more usual work, painted on copper and involving a great amount of detail, but there are also one or two more delicate works, showing the artist's draughtmanship. Room 9 includes a portrait of San Carlo Borromeo, one of the greatest of Milanese churchmen. San Carlo was apparently too ugly to have been anything except a saint, and the portrait certainly shows him to have had a nose of 'interesting' shape and proportions; and perhaps the artist was being flattering!

Room 11 contains a work by the young Caravaggio, a fruit basket, now believed to be the earliest still life completed in Italy. For its time it really is an extraordinary painting. From a much later time there are also a number of works by the contemporary Milanese artist Gaetano Sperati.

Sculpture is also represented at the gallery, with work from several centuries. The bronze Neapolitan girl by Vincenzo Gemito is a particularly fine exhibit.

The library of the Ambrosiana contains items as rare as the gallery. Not the show, but part of the collection, is a series of notes and autographed drawings by Leonardo, known as the *Codice Atlantico*, a total of twelve volumes which measured 64.5 by 43.5 centimetres. Other rare items include a fifth-century illustrated homer text, the *Ilias Picta*, a very early version of the *Divine Comedy*, and a fine collection of Books of Hours.

(Please note that in early 1990 the Ambrosiana closed for major renovation work that was expected to take as long as 12 months. It is possible that when it reopens the ordering of rooms may be different from that outlined above. There is no suggestion that any of the art itself will be moved from the building.)

From the Ambrosiana go down Via Cantù to reach Via

North to the Castle

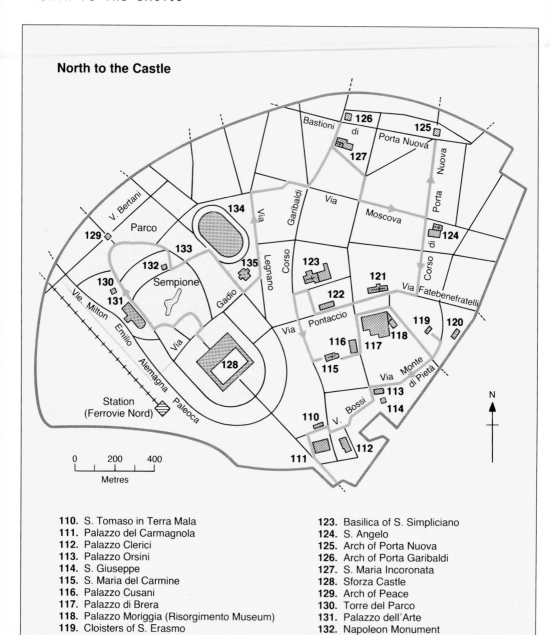

110. S. Tomaso in Terra Mala
111. Palazzo del Carmagnola
112. Palazzo Clerici
113. Palazzo Orsini
114. S. Giuseppe
115. S. Maria del Carmine
116. Palazzo Cusani
117. Palazzo di Brera
118. Palazzo Moriggia (Risorgimento Museum)
119. Cloisters of S. Erasmo
120. Palazzo Borromeo D'Adda
121. S. Marco
122. Palazzo Crivelli

123. Basilica of S. Simpliciano
124. S. Angelo
125. Arch of Porta Nuova
126. Arch of Porta Garibaldi
127. S. Maria Incoronata
128. Sforza Castle
129. Arch of Peace
130. Torre del Parco
131. Palazzo dell'Arte
132. Napoleon Monument
133. Fontana sulfurea
134. Arena
135. Acquarium

North to the Castle

The Sforza Castle
In the mid-fourteenth-century Galeazzo Visconti decided to build a fortress at the north-western end of the city, incorporating the existing town wall and a gate in it – the Porta Giovia – into his new castle. Later members of the Visconti family added to and remodelled the existing structure, maintaining the defined idea that this was a castle not a residence. Only with Filippo Maria Visconti did the castle become a *palazzo* as well as a *castello*, with certain changes being made to accommodate the dukes in the style to which they had become accustomed. When Filippo died, however, the Milanese, seeing the huge *palazzo* less now as a symbol of their protection and more one of their subjugation, demolished a large part of it.

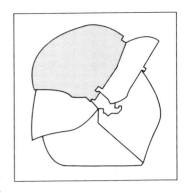

The Clock Tower entrance, Sforza Castle

When Francesco Sforza came to power in 1450, he was required to start virtually from scratch in his quest for a fortress home. To Sforza we owe the plan of the present building, his use of the great architects of the day, chiefly Il Filarete, ensuring that the *castello* became one of the great monuments of Renaissance architecture. Later Ludovico il Moro commisioned Leonardo to carry out work on the building in addition to completing his fresco of the Last Supper at Santa Maria delle Grazie.

Unfortunately, following the death of Ludovico the castle went into serious decline. A gunpowder explosion – as a result of a lightning strike – brought down Il Filarete's tower, while later occupation by the Spaniards meant the loss of many of the domestic parts of the structure as it reverted to its role of being a garrison fortress. When Napoleon took possession of the castle he demolished much of the Spanish work, and made unstable more besides, and then following the Five Days, when Marshal Radeztsky was besieged in the castle, the Marshal knocked down several of the remaining towers, presumably afraid of their use by a rampaging city mob. By the end of the nineteenth-century the castle was in such a state that it was decided to demolish it totally. A contemporary writer claimed that it was 'a gloomy...mass, stupidly enormous and boringly uniform'.

Big it most certainly was. When the French King, Francis I, came to Milan as the new lord of northern Italy, a travelling historian wrote that the castle 'is one hundred and thirteen paces in length, in width, from the entrance door by which the King entered, it is one hundred and eight, not counting the porticoes'. The same writer was impressed too by the castle's defensive potential and its economic value. It was, he said, 'of inestimable worth and wonderfully diverse in its magnificence, its fortification, drawbridges, towers, precincts, so that its value cannot be calculated'.

Despite this assessment in October 1515, by 1893 what was left of it was to be pulled down. Fortunately, a group of interested Milanese argued the castle's case, and the architect Luca Beltrami was given the job of renovating the heap instead. He was magnificently successful, restoring the castle to its full Renaissance glory, so accurately that many visitors – and indeed many Milanese – are not aware of the fact that the castle is not four hundred years old, but one hundred.

Pride of place must go to the tower of Il Filarete, the element of the castle that dominates views of it from the city side. This tower – also known as the Torre dell'Orologio, the Clock Tower – is 70 metres high and is a perfect replica of that destroyed by gunpowder. The tower, with its tiered structure, each tier separated from the next by a roof of crenallations, is a masterpiece. The bas-relief is of Umberto I on horseback by Luigi Secchi.

Around the central tower the castle forms a rectangle of about 200 metres on a side. The four corners are formed by shorter but more massive towers, the two city side ones being circular, the two parkside ones being square (although their form is more difficult to discern as those corners of the castle are building-filled). Around the walls – and note here that these, as with the rest of the castle, are entirely brick-built – is a moat.

Passing through the clock tower an inner court is reached, a huge area that was the parade ground for the Sforza army. This

The inner fortress, Sforza Castle

189

courtyard is today used for occasional exhibitions of sculpture. The court is separated from the next section of the castle by a dead moat, that is one that was never filled. Over the bridge is the Ducal Court. The right-hand section of this now holds the Castle museum, the left section, the Roccheta, being reached through a fine doorway. The Rocchetta was the last defence, a castle within a castle. It is built around a central courtyard, arcaded on three sides. The rooms of the Rocchetta hold a collection of historical archives, the Trivulzio Library – brought here from Palazzo Trivulzio – and a section of the Milan Archaeology Museum. That section includes items on local prehistory and the Egyptian collection. The prehistory section includes items from the Paleolithic culture, from the lake dwellers of the lakes around Varese, and from the Golasecca, the late Bronze/early Iron Age culture from the southern end of Lake Maggiore.

The Castle Museum extends through the old ducal rooms, and the rooms themselves are as much a part of the museum as the collection. Here is what is believed to be the finest collection of musical instruments in Europe, with over 600 individual pieces, including some very early items from the fifteenth-century. There

is one piece by Gaspara de Salò, the resident of Salò on the western side of Lake Garda who is usually credited with having invented the violin.

The collection of arms and armour is, not surprisingly for a former garrison, comprehensive, and there are fine collections of furniture, tapestries, ivory, gold, glass and ceramics. The rooms that enclose the collections include the Sala delle Asse, the Room of Beams, which is frescoed with intertwining oak branches. The work was carried out for Ludovico il Moro by Leonardo da Vinci, but had all but disappeared as a result of damp problems by the early part of the twentieth-century. Enrico Rusca carried out a complete repair based on the last vestiges, a restoration that was much criticized at the time. Now it is hard to say whether the work is by Leonardo or Rusca.

The museum also contains a fine collection of painting and sculpture, the former including work by Il Bergagnone, Cerano, Mantegna and Tintoretto. Of the sculpture, the equestrian statue of Bernabo Visconti by Bonino da Campione is believed to be a masterpiece of its period. Pride of place must, however, go to the Pietà Rondanini of Michelangelo. Few today doubt the genius of

The Pietà of Michelangelo, Castle Museum

The Armoury Room in the Castle Museum

Michelangelo, and this is his only work in Milan. It was also his last. Many who see it believe that this was because he died before its completion but that was not the case. In reality, at the end of his life Michelangelo began to doubt if man could ever successfully capture God in either paint or stone. He therefore gave up his own attempts, afraid that they were doomed to failure, and the Pietà remained unfinished. In some ways we should be grateful, for although it would have been wonderful to have seen the completed work, it is equally wonderful to see the way in which the artist was able to draw the sculpture out of the stone. It lends a certain credence to the oft-stated idea that Michelangelo was able to see works within the stone and merely had to knock off the unwanted sections.

After visiting the museum you can exit through the rear wall of the castle, pausing one last time to look along the walls. This really is the most impressive of buildings.

Parco Sempione Beyond the castle is Parco Sempione, Milan's biggest park. At one time Sempione was part of a great ducal hunting park attached to the castle. The present form of the park was laid down in 1894 when the land was organized into gardens and woods, together with roads and piazzas, a lake and an artificial hill. Today it is the weekend meeting point for the youth of the city. On weekdays the park is cool and quiet.

Cross the small vendor-crowded piazza and head across the park to reach the small lake in which giant carp swim and, at most times in the summer, frogs croak. From here the view to the Arch of Peace is excellent, with its foreground of water and uninterrupted view along an avenue of trees seemingly chosen for their colour match.

Begin an exploration by going to the left of the lake to reach the Palazzo dell'Arte, a huge building built in 1931 and given to the city by the industrialist Bernocchi al Comune. Since that donation the *palazzo* has been the permanent headquarters of the Triennale di Milano, a fair which takes place every three years. The aim of the fair, held in the *palazzo* and its grounds, is to integrate art with everyday life by way of meetings and exhibitions.

Next is the Torre del Parco, a steel tower 108 metres high, and no taller out of respect for the Madonnina on the Duomo (although the TV mast added in 1952 is actually higher than the

Bottom
Parco Sempione

Left
The Arch of Peace

Below
Detail of the Arch of Peace

statue). The tower is reached from outside the park and was built in 1933 to give the public a chance to admire their city. The view is reached by lift up the central steel tube.

The *Arco della Pace*, the arch of Peace, that stands at the head of the park, is set in a building-free circle that allows a full appreciation of its elegant lines. The arch was designed by Luigi Cagnola to celebrate the victories of Napoleon and erected in 1807 as the Arco delle Vittorie. When the Austrians re-entered the city in 1815 the arch was hastily redesigned in certain areas and renamed. The new Arco delle Pace was inaugurated in 1838 by Ferdinando of Austria in 1838, by which time Cagnola had been dead for five years, which is a great shame. After each of the next two victorious marches into the city, by Napoleon III and Vittorio Emanuele II, the arch was further modified, although it retained its title.

The monument is largely of marble and is of conventional Roman triumphal arch design, now known principally for its use in the Parisian *Arc de Triomphe*. It is, in face, three arches, supported by Corinthian columns and decorated with numerous allegorical designs. The semi-reclining figures near the top – two on each side of the arch – represent the rivers Fiumi, Po, Ticino and Tagliamento.

On the top of the arch the *Sestiga della Pace*, the six-horsed Chariot of Peace, is by Abbondio Sangiorgio, while the flanking *Vittorie a Cavallo*, Victories on Horseback, are by Giovanni Putti. Originally the chariot was going to face Paris, a fact that some say pleased Napoleon while others say it was at his insistence, but it was turned around when the lordship of the city changed hands again.

Recently it was discovered – or rediscovered – that the arch has rooms inside it and that these are connected to each other and to the top by steps and ladders. Work is now under way to open the arch to visitors. When that happens it will be one of the foremost tourist spots in the city; the idea of absorbing the view of the Sforza Castle over the Sempione Park is mouth-watering.

From the arch we head back into the park to see the monument to Napoleon, a masterpiece by Luigi Canonica set on an artificial hill that is known, irreverently, as 'thrush mountain' (to distinguish it from 'sparrow mountain' in the public gardens). The work was completed in 1806, but had to be kept in the courtyard of the Palazzo del Senato during the period of the Austrian re-occupation.

In the monument Napoleon is seen at the moment of his triumphal entry into Milan after the battle of Magenta.

Beyond the monument, leave the park through the gated exit to the left; the area you reach is still parkland, Sempione ending gradually on this north-eastern border. To the right as you exit, a few tens of metres away, is the Fontana d'Acqua Sulfurea, the 'fountain of sulphurous water'. The fountain is curious, being in form a grass-covered stone a bit like a shower head, out of which pours water smelling (stinking?) of sulphur. The Milanese, ever practical, call it *acqua marci* or 'rotten water', but claims it is good for curing kidney stones and liver complaints. As a consequence, it is frequently surrounded by people filling bottles for their own use. Whether the water is of any real benefit or merely a placebo is, perhaps, a matter of taste.

The Arena As you leave the park you will see a low, wide building directly ahead. This is the Milan Arena. It is of Neo-Classical design, although based on a Roman amphitheatre with its tiers of steps, and was built in 1806. It saw its first event in the presence of Napoleon and was used for horse-racing festivals as well, apparently, as chariot racing and mock naval battles. With the rise in popularity of football the arena became Milan's stadium, but it lost this role with the building of the Giuseppe Meazza (San Siro) stadium. Today it hosts athletics meeting and festivals.

The arena is the classical ellipse and can hold 30,000 people. In keeping with the Roman design, the arena has two large triumphal doors at the heads of the long axis of the ellipse, and two smaller doors at the heads of the short axis. Each of these smaller doors is known as the *Porta Libitnaria*, the 'Door of the grave-diggers' (from the Latin *libitini*), because in Roman times the dead gladiators were removed through them.

Finally, at the right end of the arena, as you first saw it, is the city aquarium. This was built in 1906 for the International Exhibition which took place in Milan. There are about forty tanks full of fish and crustaceans, and some reptiles, together with a library and some research facilities for scientists. The frontage of the building is dominated by a statue of Neptune, the god in a very severe mood, almost daring you not to enter his kingdom.

Santa Maria Incoronata Go along the city edge of the arena, enjoying the shade of the trees that form a fine avenue beside the Via Legnano, to reach Piazza Lega Lombarda. Go right and across this to reach Via Porta Tenaglia and follow this to the square of Lago La Foppa. Northward out of the square, Corso Garibaldi reaches the arch of Porta Garibaldi. This was erected in 1826 in honour of Emperor Francis I of Austria's entry into Milan in the previous year. The not inconsiderable cost of the arch was covered by Lombard shopkeepers, as a plaque thoughtfully reminds us. The other dedications, to Garibaldi, the *Eroe dei Due Mondi* or 'Hero of the two worlds', were added when the arch was re-dedicated in 1859. As with the Arch of Peace the design is Roman, with the large central opening and two smaller side arches. At the top the reclining figures again symbolize rivers, although in this case they are the same on both sides.

Return down Corso Garibaldi to reach the church of Santa Maria Incoronato, St Mary Crowned. This comprises twin Renaissance-style buildings; that on the left was built in 1451 by Francesco Sforza, while that on the right followed nine years later, Sforza's wife, Bianca Maria being responsible. The whole is supposed to symbolize the perfect marital union of the couple. Whether that harmony was because the two liked each other, or whether it was rather what they represented - he the first Sforza duke, she the last descendant of the last Visconti duke – is less clear. What is known is that Bianca Maria wanted her church dedicated to San Nicola da Tolentiono, intending there to be twin dedication, to go with twin altars, and so on. However, only the façades are twinned, the inside of the building being common. And there is just one dedication, although the bas-reliefs above the doors do show San Nicola as well as the Virgin.

Beside the church was an Augustinian monastery which was rich and powerful until it was disbanded in 1798, its buildings then being taken over as a barracks, then as a prison and finally as a school.

The church was refaced several times during this period, but is now being slowly restored to its original form. Inside, the fine fresco of Jesus struggling with the cross while his blood is caught in a gold vessel has been attributed to both Zenale and Ambrogio da Fossano (Il Bergognone), neither as yet having the edge in terms of weight of critical opinion. The second chapel to the left has frescoes which show episodes from the Milanese plague, while the vault fresco of St Anthony is widely believed to by be Zenale.

196

The third chapel on the right holds the tombs of both Matteo Bossi and Antonio Landriani, while the second chapel holds that of Archbishop Gabriele Sforza.

Go down Via Marsala beside the church. In Via Milazza to the left here is the restaurant Giallo, at No. 6. This pleasant, happy place is not always open at lunchtime; it is worth returning in the early evening.

Stone doves, San Francesco's Fountain, Piazza San Angelo

Church of Sant' Angelo Continue down Via Marsala and go right into Via Solferino where it ends. At the junction with Via Moscova go left and follow the road to reach the church of Sant' Angelo. The church stands in a delightful tree-shrouded piazza in which sits the fountain of San Francesco. This delight is the work of Giannino Castiglioni and was completed in 1927. St Francis of Assissi is shown talking to the birds on, and the fish in, the pool. So life-like are the carved birds that from a distance it is difficult to tell which are the real ones taking advantage of the fountain's fresh water.

The church of Sant' Angelo was built to replace an earlier one known as Santa Maria degli Angioli which had been pulled down by governor Ferrante Gonzaga in order to make way for a new city wall. It was deconsecrated in the mid-nineteenth-century, but has been reconsecrated and opened for worship.

Externally the church is, frankly, dull but inside it has numerous excellent frescoes including many by Camillo Procaccini and several by Pietro, the son of Bernardino Luini.

North of the church, reached along Corso di Porta Nuovo itself, is the Arch of Porta Nuova, though frankly the detour is hardly worthwhile. As with the Arch of Peace this arch was erected to celebrate the victories of Napoleon. It was completed in 1813, but as it was built in a very fragile stone it has not weathered at all well and has needed a great deal of restoration which has hardly improved its appearance.

Via Fatebenefratelli Better than making that detour towards the city centre, going along Corso di Porta Nuova away from the arch and turning right into Via Fatebenefratelli when the crossroads is reached. This new road is superb, an ancient, high and narrow street that gives a flavour of older Milan. Along it, to the right, is the church of San Marco. This was built in the mid-thirteenth-century by the Milanese nobleman Lanfranco Settala

197

who had become head of the adjacent monastery of the Hermits of St Augustine. It is said that the dedication was in appreciation of the efforts of the Venetians in the rebuilding of the city after it had been destroyed by Barbarossa. The church is very vast. Like that of San Lorenzo it looks like a small village when viewed from the side, with its long array of chapels of varying heights, each with circular windows and shallow roof caps. These chapels were built by, or for, other nobles, although the statuary and memorials of the nobles that once graced them have long gone, dispersed after San Carlo Borromeo enacted the decision of the Council of Trent that such things should not be tolerated. The campanile of this church was also shortened by Ferrante Gonzaga because it overtopped the castle defences.

Externally, the church shows little now of its origins, and only the fine front door is really obvious. For the rest it is pseudo-Gothic, although that should not be seen as a derogatory comment, especially about the central window which is wonderful.

Inside, the first chapel on the right, Capella Foppa, is beautifully decorated. Sadly this was the last work of the artist Paolo Lomazzo,

Via Fatebenefratelli

who went blind at the age of 33. On the left wall of the chapel the fresco of the fall of Simon is believed to be the artist's masterpiece. The fourth chapel is known as the Chapel of the Crucifix because of the very rare eighteenth-century wooden crucifix held there.

Elsewhere the church, which has numbered among its congregation the very young Martin Luther and Mozart, holds the sarcophagus of the founder, and, in the presbytery, two paintings by established masters, an argument between Sant' Ambrogio and Sant' Agostino – a seemingly odd choice of subject – by Camillo Procaccini and a Baptism of Sant' Agostino by Battista Crespi. Finally, be sure to see a black and white fresco in the eighth bay of the north transept. This was only discovered in 1975 and is attributed to the Leonardo school, although not (as yet, at least) to the master himself.

Next along Via Fatebenefratelli is Palazzo Crivelli. This fine *palazzo* was built for the Marquis Crivelli in the seventeenth-century. The long façade was even longer when the *palazzo* was first built and is noticeable for the wrought-iron balcony which breaks up an otherwise severe, although nicely coloured, exterior.

Oriel window, church of San Marco

Inside, the *palazzo's* courtyard is arcaded, supported by Tuscan granite columns. The *palazzo* also holds another contender for Milan's best staircase, a double stonework stairway in flamboyant Baroque style.

Basilica of San Simplicano Go right now, into Via San Simplicano, to reach one of the gems of this northern section of the city. The basilica of San Simplicano is one of the oldest foundations in Milan, having been started by Sant' Ambrogio on, it is believed, the site of a pagan cemetery. It was the last of the four basilicas that Sant' Ambrogio built – Sant' Ambrogio, San Nazaro and the long-gone San Dionigi being the others – and was originally called the Basilica of the Virgins. The church was

The Basilica of San Simplicano

completed by Sant' Ambrogio's successor, San Simpliciano, who later became Pope (from 397–401). The saint wished to be buried in the church and when he was, the dedication was changed. Nothing of that early church survives. Indeed, very little of any of the churches that appeared on the site now survives, and the central doorway of the façade is from the twelfth-century, so comprehensive was the rebuilding in the late nineteenth-century. However, restoration work of the original plan is underway and it would appear that in form San Simpliciano is one of the most complete of Milan's early sacred sites.

At the time of San Simpliciano the church received the relics of three martyrs from the Val di Non, Saints Sisinnio, Martirio and Alessandro, which were interred in a common funerary urn. For many years the church was a place of pilgrimage because of the relics, but the veneration increased dramatically after a miraculous event in 1176. On 29 May, the day of the battle of Legnano, three white doves were seen to struggle free of the reliquary urn and fly up to the top of the church. This was viewed as a sign that the army of the Lombard League would defeat that of Barbarossa. This it duly did. Today, this miracle is still celebrated in the church, on the last Sunday in May.

Externally the church is Romanesque in style, the two smaller side doors having decoration depicting the wise and foolish virgins, a link with Sant' Ambrogio's original dedication. The church's campanile, built of old tombstones in its lower section, was shortened to 25 metres in 1552 by order of Ferrante Gonzaga because it overtopped the castle defences and so represented a hazard.

Restoration work in the church in 1976 revealed a Renaissance fresco in the first chapel on the right, although the masterpiece of the church is still believed to be the vault fresco showing the Coronation of the Virgin by Il Bergonone. In the crowd of onlookers the figure on the right is said to be of Dante. Below the organ, in galleries of the presbytery, are frescoed saints by Aurelio Luini, son of the great master.

Santa Maria Del Carmine to Palazzo di Brera

South from San Simpliciano another fine church, Santa Maria del Carmine, is reached by returning to the main road – Via Fatebenefratelli has now become Via Pontaccio – going right

The bells of the campanile of the Church of San Simplicanio were said to possess healing qualities, although the oft-repeated story of a Milanese merchant's toothache does not necessarily reinforce this view. The man is said to have asked permission of the church to pull the bell rope by attaching it to his teeth. Permission was granted, but the merchant, not understanding the pulling power of a tumbling bell, could not save himself from being hauled off his feet and having his head comprehensively bashed on the ceiling above. Apparently, this cured his toothache...

201

**The Church and Piazza of
Santa Maria del Carmine**

along it, then left down Via Mercato. The church is delightfully set in a quiet, café-edged piazza, hidden when you first reach the square behind a large and thought-provoking modern sculpture.

This church was erected in the second half of the fifteenth-century next to a house of Carmelite nuns, although the façade, in the most beautiful pseudo-Gothic style, dates only from the last century. The campanile is seventeenth-century, but was shortened in the following century because the Austrian city governor felt it dominated the castle and represented a threat. Since this is the third church so far whose campanile has suffered that fate, it must be assumed that the governor had a miserable life, spending his time in despair at the thought of being attacked.

To get inside the church – after a long, long look at that exquisite façade – the visitor has to go down half a dozen steps, so much has the city street level risen in the centuries since the original building was raised. Inside, the chapel of the Madonna of Carmel has fine works in marble and canvases by Camillo Procaccini. A door, elsewhere in the church, gives access to the nunnery cloisters and a close-up view of the campanile.

From the church go along Via del Carmine at its right-hand side to reach, at the corner of that road with Via Brera, the Palazzo Cusani. This is now part of the Army Headquarters, but it was built for the Marquis of Casani and was once one of the centres for Milanese artistic and intellectual life in the eighteenth-century, a position it continued to hold for most of the time of Austrian dominance. The façade of the building is luxuriously decorated with delightful balconies and crests. There are two identical doors, the story being that each of the two Cusani brothers wanted his own entrance. Outside the *palazzo* the fine rearing horse is a bronze by Aligi Sassu.

Go left along Via Brera to reach the Palazzo di Brerea, which should be one of the great showpieces of Milan – a *palazzo* in fine style housing a superb art collection. Unfortunately, the Brera has had financial difficulties of late, and has also become home ground to a group of students who have taken to despoiling the building with posters and graffiti. Perhaps some valid point is being made and justice is on the side of the students, but I do wish they had left this stately building alone. Rumour now is that following some refurbishment work all will be well; I hope so.

Right
Statue to Napoleon, Palazzo Brera

Below
Detail of the statue to Napoleon, Palazzo Brera

The *palazzo* is grand-style Baroque, and has a unity that is in strong contrast to the fact that its erection took over 100 years, starting in the sixteenth-century. It was built on the site of a former convent of the Sisters of Humility. The convent itself had been built on a piece of scrub land which had taken the name *braida*, a Germanic word for such a site. This was Italianized to *brera*, a name that has stuck. The sisterhood was suppressed by San

204

Carlo Borromeo, and the site passed to the Jesuits who had the *palazzo* built. In it the Order set up a library, an observatory and a school. When that Order too was suppressed in 1773, an initiative by Maria Teresa of Austria resulted in a fine arts academy being set up in the *palazzo*; this became the famous 'Pinacoteca'. In 1780 the architect Giuseppe Piermarini added the Neo-Classical doorway to the façade.

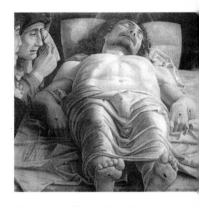

The *Dead Christ* of Andreas Mantegna, Brera Museum

Behind the façade is a wonderful courtyard, a masterpiece by Richini. The courtyard is defined by two-tier arcades, each arch held up by twin granite columns. At the centre of the courtyard is a bronze of Napoleon representing him as a demi-god in victorious pose. The bronze, a very fine piece, is the work of the great Antonio Canova.

The Brera collection is excellent and includes works by Bernardino Luini, Raphael, Titian, Tintoretto, Bellini, Foppi and Ferrari. Pride of place must go, however, to the Madonna with Saints and Federico di Montelfeltro by Piero della Francesco, which has gained international renown for its near-perfect representation of perspective and form, and the Dead Christ of Andreas Mantegna. It is difficult to view the latter without feeling a sense of shock. The work was completed in 1480, yet the composition, sombre colour and vivid realism are almost modern.

The Brera has recently been extended to include the Jesi donation and a loan of the Jucker collection so that, in addition to the Renaissance Lombard art, there are also works by Picasso and Modigliani.

Sharing the building with the Pinacoteca is the Braidense National Library, as started by Maria Teresa of Austria around the library of the Jesuits. There are over a million documents, books and pamphlets here, including all the Milanese newspapers from the Napoleonic era and over 2,000 rare ancient volumes. The collection extends to works on history, philosophy and the social sciences.

The *Accademia di Belle Arti* on the same site is also a foundation of Maria Teresa, now a famous school covering all aspects of art and architecture. The academy also runs evening classes for those wanting to study the arts, and has a fine collection of pictures, sculptures and set designs.

The Brera's Astronomic Observatory numbers among past scholars Giovanni Schiaparelli, who discovered the 'canals' of

Mars. The observatory still has study programmes in meteorology, seismology and astronomy.

The Final Leg From the Brera continue up Via Brera, then go right along Via Fiori Oscuri, walking along the northern wall of Palazzo Brera, and go right into Via Borgonuovo. There, tucked into the rear of the Palazzo Brera, is Palazzo Moriggia. This *palazzo* is of Renaissance origin, but was reworked by Piermarini for the Marquis Moriggia in 1775. After many owners it passed to the city and now houses the Risorgimento Museum. Externally the *palazzo* is elegant, with a fine balcony and mouldings, but it is the museum that is really interesting.

The Risorgimento Museum – the Risorgimento is the name given to the reawakening of the sense of Italian identity and the struggle for re-unification of the country – covers the period from Napoleon's First Italian Campaign in 1796 through to the liberation of Rome in 1870. The fourteen rooms are laid out in strict chronological sequence, so anyone wanting, for instance, to concentrate on the history of Garibaldi's Thousand can go directly to Rooms 9–12. There you can see Garibaldi's cloak, his hat and his medals. In the room devoted to the *Cinque Giornate*, the Five Days, is the bell of the Broletto which broke with the effort of five day's toil.

Good though the museum is, you will need a fair knowledge of Italian to get the best from it. For those who do not speak the language well there is a fine series of paintings – the struggles for Italian unity in pictures – and an interesting collection of flags, including rare ones of the Cisalpine Republic.

At the bottom of Via Borgonuovo the visitor arrives at a new city fountain erected when the new Line 3 Metro station (Montenapoleono – but beware, some maps list it as Manzoni, which was the originally proposed name) was pierced on Piazza Croce Rossa. The fountain is interesting, although a better choice of material or colouring might have prevented the top lintel from looking quite so much like a rusty RSJ.

Here you have a choice, although not one route to the positive exclusion of the other. One choice is to go left along Via dei Giardini, then left into a quiet, be-flowered cul-de-sac to see what remains of the cloisters of Sant' Erasmo. Part of the apartment block across the back wall of the small square is all that is left of the cloisters of the convent church of Sant' Erasmo built in the fifteenth and sixteenth-centuries. The cloister arcades are held aloft by columns with Renaissance capitals.

Go back out of the cul-de-sac and over Via dei Giardini to Via Pisoni. Go down this to Via Manzoni and left there to see the Palazzo Borromeo-D'Adda, whose frontage is so long that it covers two numbers of the road. Although the *palazzo* was clearly built on a grand scale it is beautifully simple, its only concessions to grandness being the columned and balconied doorway and the final flourish way up above the door. Inside there are three courtyards and some of the rooms are, apparently, exquisite.

If, instead of going left along Via Manzoni you had gone right you would soon have reached Via Giuseppe Verdi to the left. On the corner is the Palazzo Orsini, built in the late sixteenth-century, although the family Orsini who were responsible for the building soon moved to another house. A door from the original construction is now housed in the castle Museum. Through the doorway once closed by that door is a fine Renaissance courtyard which some say is the work of Il Pellegrini, while others say is the work of his rival for the title of best architect in Milan, Galeazzo Alessi.

A little further along Via Verdi is the church of San Giuseppe. This was the work of a young architect who was to go on to make a mark on Italian architecture, Francesco Maria Richinim, and the youthfulness of its creator can be seen in its bold changes of angle and decorative twirls. Inside there is an ornate rococo altar with statues and shields and several fine seventeenth-century paintings.

Opposite Palazzo Orsini and San Giuseppe, and bisecting them, is Via Boito. Take this, and Via Bossi that is a continuation of it, to reach, to the left, Via Clerici with its *palazzo* of the same name.

Palazzo Clerici is a superb rococo house, one of the best – along with Palazzo Litta in Corso Magenta – of its style in the City. Originally the home of the Marquis Giorgio Clerici, who had the interior decorated by the best artists of the day, including Tiepolo – whose best work has the long, if specific title, *The World Illuminated by the Chariot of the Sun Driven by Mercury* – the house was eventually used by the Archduke of Austria, and became the Court of Appeal when it was taken over the city in

1816. Today it is the headquarters of the Institute for International Political Studies.

The *palazzo* is set back from the line of the street so that carriages could more easily set down and pick up their passengers, and betrays little evidence on the outside of the luxurious nature of its interior.

At the end of Via Bossi go right, then first left into Via San Tomaso. To the right here is the church of San Tomaso in Terra Mala. This Neo-Classical church – actually built in the late sixteenth-century but revamped in the early years of the nineteenth-century – is notable for its side-chapel paintings. These include another rendering of San Carlo Borromeo, here rising into heaven, the work of Giulio Cesare Procaccini, an artist of the early seventeenth-century, and of St Mary Magelene

Piazza Cordusio

adoring Christ, by Antonio Campi, an artist of the last years of the sixteenth-century.

Go right at the end of Via San Tomaso into Via Rovello and follow this past Palazzo del Carmagnola. This fifteenth-century *palazzo* was given to the *condottiero* Francesco Bussone (known as *Il Carmagnola*) by Filippo Maria Visconti. Unfortunately Il Carmagnola was a real *condottiero*, a mercenary, who left Milan to serve Venice and, as a consequence, lost the *palazzo*. It is probable that Bussone shed few tears over the loss as repossession of the house would have swiftly resulted in the loss of his head. After Bussone the *palazzo* was used by Cecilia Gallerani, a consort of Ludovico il Moro, and was the focal point of Milanese high society. Leonardo and Bramante were both guests here. Foreign domination caused a decline and the *palazzo,* in a poor state of health, was given to the city which used it at first as a granary. Finally it was used as the *broletto,* being known as the *Broletto Nuovissimo,* the 'very new *broletto*'. Today it houses the local tax office.

In the entrance is a plaque to the former owner. Beyond are two courtyards, the second and larger of which opens on to Via Broletto. The four-sided arcade here is superb.

Go left along Via Dante, pausing only to look back along the length of the street to the castle, your starting point, to reach the Piazza Cordusio, a huge, elliptical 'square' built only a century ago, despite being only a stone's throw from the Duomo. The name derives from the *Curia Ducis*, the Duke's Court; here at one time stood the Court of Lombardy Dukes. Today it is the home of banks and insurance houses. The monument at the centre is to Giuseppe Parini, the work of Luigi Secchi in 1889.

From the Cordusio, as it is usually known, a short walk past Piazza dei Mercanti leads back to the Piazza del Duomo.

The Outer City

The Pirelli Tower From almost any part of the city, and especially from the roof of the Duomo, the view north is dominated by the Pirelli Tower. The tower is 124 metres (about 405 feet high), nearly 16 metres (about 50 feet) higher than the Madonnina on the Duomo. It was built in the late 1950s for the Pirelli company (of tyre and calendar fame), and is an elegant structure, looking like a point-free sword, narrowing towards the edges. Ironically, the quite small area on which the tower stands – small for its height, that is – is approximately the same as that for the first factory that Giovan Battista Pirelli set up.

The Pirelli Tower

Today, the tower no longer belongs to the company, and is an administrative centre for the Region of Lombardy, but is still known by its former name. The view from the terrace at the top of the tower is extensive, and can occasionally be shared by the visitor. Ring 67651 and ask for an access permit. If you do not have such a permit, do not bother to turn up at the tower; security is tight and you will not be allowed in.

The Central Station In the shadow of the Pirelli Tower is Milan's Central Station, a huge building built in the mid-1920s. A few years later and the style of the building could well have been Lictorian (Fascist), but in fact the station was constructed in grand style. The frontage is over 200 metres long and 36 metres high, and apart from its vast porticoes, it has elegant, if elongated statues. The winged horses are excellent, but look too for the wolf suckling Romulus and Remus, a rather strange work for an Italian city other than Rome. The gargoyle faces at the edges of the frontage used to gargle water into the fountain basins below, but they have been dry for some time now.

On the sides of the building the grand style continues with more elaborate decoration, but the real surprise is to be found inside. For a start the visitor finds that the frontage is false, and

Statue on the Central Station

211

there is another covered frontage within what is a covered vehicle access area. Through the huge doorways the grand style continues: the ticket office is the size of an aircraft hangar, while the stairway that goes up to the platforms – yes, up; the platforms and trains are at a higher level than the road – still has a majestic sweep if you ignore the newer escalators.

At platform level is the Museo delle Cere, the Wax Museum, a series of tableaux of personages and events in world history.

Close to the station, at No.4 Via Andrea Doria, which goes diagonally right away from the Piazzale Duca d'Aosta (when viewing the station), is Palazzo Pozzobonelli. This fine house, now surrounded by modern buildings, was built in the fifteenth-century, in what was then the country, for a noble Milanese family. Externally, the *palazzo* has little enough to detain the visitor, but inside it has, some claim, a place in the history of the city. A mural in one of the rooms is said to have given Luca Beltrami the form of the Filarete Tower on the castle that allowed him to reconstruct it to its original glory. However, as you will soon see, there is another claimant to that honour.

The Idroscalo To the east of the city, near Linate, is the Idroscalo, built in the late 1920s for use by seaplanes but now given over to watersports enthusiasts. Swimmers can use a small beach, the Riviera of Milan – the city's name for it, not mine – while windsurfing, sailing, water-skiing and fishing are all possible.

If you want a quieter spot for bathing or fishing, try the Laghetto Redecesio, a flooded quarry complex a little north of, and city-side of, the Idroscalo.

Abbey of Chiaravalle South of the city, and reached from the Rogoredo exit of the Tangentiale, is the Abbey of Chiaravalle. The abbey was founded in 1135 when St Bernard of Clairvaux brought a group of the newly-founded Cisterican Order to this spot. The Cistercians are famous for having founded their monastic houses in wild, beautiful areas, and for their agricultural innovations. Here, it is said, there was a swamp before the monks arrived, but they drained it, turning the area into fertile farmland.

Of the first Cistercian building nothing now remains, although there are significant remains from later remodelling, some of that work being by Bramante. Sadly, the abbey suffered humiliations in middle life. The Cisalpine Republic suppressed the Cistercians and soon after the buildings themselves started to be demolished, although this happened piecemeal over a number of years. The saddest act was the demolition in 1861 of Bramante's cloister in order to make way for the railway line from Milan to Genoa. Thankfully, full demolition was prevented after the abbey was taken over by an interested owner. The abbey was gradually renovated and then, in 1952, it was returned to the Cistercian Order who have continued the work of restoration.

The entrance to the abbey buildings is through an archway in the upper level of which are a chapel, to the left, and a church, to the right. The chapel, a fifteenth-century building, was for women visitors to the abbey (women were not allowed to enter the grounds). The church was for visitors, who stayed in the guest room beside it.

The abbey church façade is split horizontally at about half-height, the lower section being Baroque – rebuilt Baroque, that is – while the upper section is reconstructed Romanesque. The combination has technical interest but the two halves are too dissimilar to be totally in harmony. To the right of the abbey the campanile is sixteenth-century, although the clock is earlier. Above the façade rises the magnificent tower, the jewel of the abbey buildings. Built in the fourteenth-century, the tower, with its white marble columns, its tiers, and its final spire with its spherical capping, is among the most elegant structures in Milan, perhaps the only rival to the campanile of San Gottardo.

Beside the church there was once a cemetery in which were buried some of the rich and famous of Milanese society. The bodies were re-interred in the eighteenth-century, but some of the tombs and headstones remain. Here you will find memorials to Pagano della Torre, the first Duke of Milan, to the Viscontis and, as a complete change, to Guglielmina La Boema, a thirteenth-century witch claimed by some to have been so powerful that the church dared not confront her. Whether that is true or not is a matter of debate, but it is true that she died of natural causes, and that her body was burned at the stake only after her death.

Inside the church what catches the eye is the woodcarving of the choir stalls. The story goes that Carlo Garavaglia was being

213

hunted by the law for having killed his brother and that he sought sanctuary in the abbey. In time he repented his sins and became a monk, a part of the penance agreed by his fellow monks was to carve the stalls with scenes from the life of St Bernard. The stalls are now seen as one of the masterpieces of seventeenth-century woodcarving. Elsewhere, note the painting of the Madonna and Child by Bernardino Luini at the top of the blind stairway that once led to the monk's dormitory. The work is one of Luini's earliest, and was known as the Madonna of the Good Night, because the monks passed it each time they retired to bed!

Finally, go outside again to see the thirteenth-century cloister, actually rebuilt since the end of World War II. The memorial plaques are to the founding and consecration of the abbey. The chapterhouse, reached from the eastern side of the cloister, has three famous frescoes of Milan. One shows the Duomo being built, another Santa Maria delle Grazie, also under construction, while the third shows the castle. It is this fresco that some say give Luca Beltrami his view of the Filarate Tower rather than that in the Palazzo Pozzobonelli.

The Canals Continuing around Milan clockwise, you reach an area where the ancient canals of the city remain intact and water-filled. The earliest canals were built in part as a means of defence against Barbarossa, although they were soon expanded for trade, initially for the bringing in of building marble for the Duomo, and later for more straightforward commerce. Soon the canals were being built up so that they looked Venetian, and in the older, quieter corners they still do, although on a very small scale.

into a peripheral road, although this filling happened less because the canals had outlived their usefulness and more because the lack of sea-purging, as at Venice, led to them becoming increasingly unhygenic. A growing awareness of the advantages of cleanliness led to opposition to their existence. Today in the city it is only at the Porta Ticinese that the water still forms part of the city architecture, and it is here, on the first Sunday in June, that a remnant canal festival is still celebrated.

South of the city the canals are still much as they were and the visitor with time and patience to spare — and both are needed; the Milanese canals are linear so that, unlike Venice, where a casual stroll can always be made circular, all explorations are out and back and the best bit is always likely to be around the next corner – can still find odd, delightful corners and architectural gems. One such gem, although it can hardly be said to lie among perfect canal architecture, is the church of San Cristofer sul Naviglio. This lies on the right side (the north side) of the Naviglio Grande that leaves Porta Ticinese. In truth it actually leaves from a point near the Darsena, but the Ticinese was its original final point. The right side of the canal, looking along its length from the city end, is followed by the Strada Alzaia Naviglio, and the church lies on this some 600 metres from the water's end, close to the railway bridge.

The church is actually two churches combined, the earliest one, to the left, is thirteenth-century and was originally attached to a hospice for travellers on the canal, which explains the dedication. At a later stage the hospice was converted to a church in Gothic style. The combination looks a little strange, but the building's position adds a touch of romance. Inside, there is a fine frescoed portrait of the patron saint of travellers, depicting him in the act of carrying Christ across a river, the story that lies behind his now-accepted patronage of people on the move. Each year on 25 July cars are driven past the church in procession and are blessed.

San Siro Complex Continuing clockwise around the city you reach, almost due west of the city centre, one of the finest centres for spectator sports of any city in Europe. Here, close to the Lotto stop on the Molino Dorino branch of Line 1 (red line), is the San Siro complex.

Closest to the Metro station, and the fine Piazzale Lotto into which you emerge, is Lido di Milan. The lido has two swimming pools and was Europe's largest complex when it was completed in 1930. In addition to the pools there are tennis courts, bowling greens and roller skating, together with bars, a restaurant and many tree-lined walks.

Close to the Lido is the Palazzetto dello Sport (the Palalido), a modern building usually used for sporting events but occasionally also the venue for concerts. The *palazzetto's* capacity is about 7,000.

To the other side of the Lido is the low wall of San Siro racecourse, built in 1921 for both flat and jump races. Race meetings are held from the middle of March to the middle of July and from September to November. They are never held at the same time as meetings in the nearby trotting course as there is only one set of staff, shared between the two!

The trotting stadium is reached on the other side of the racecourse, following signs to the football stadium. The course, with its one-kilometre track, was built in 1925 but radically remodelled after World War II to make it one of the best-equipped courses in Europe. There are about 200 races each year, including some night-time meetings in summer.

Beyond the Trotatoio is the football stadium, officially named the Giuseppe Meazza, but popularly known as San Siro because when it was first built, in 1926, it actually was called by that name. The stadium is the official ground of both AC Milan (known locally as Milan) and Internazionale Milan (known as Inter), which rather negates the argument frequently heard in Britain that it is impossible for teams to share grounds. Following enlarging and modernization work in 1955 the ground can now hold now 80,000 people in relative comfort. For the 1990 football World Cup the stadium as semi-roofed with a structure that looks as though it was completed from a meccano set.

The external appearance of the stadium is consistent with the position of football in Italian society. Football is king, and little expense has been spared in making the ground both functional and aesthetically attractive. The walkways that take people to the upper reaches of the ground are especially good at combining these attributes.

Beside the stadium is the Palazzo dello Sport (the Palasport), a more elegant structure than the Palalido and having a capacity of about 15,000. It was designed to cater for fourteen sports as well as concerts and was built in the early 1970s. Damaged by recent bad winter weather, the centre is still being repaired.

Finally, the non-sports enthusiast can go to Monte Stella, an artificial hill that lies to the north of the racecourse. The hill, also known as Montagnola, was built up with the rubble of bombed buildings mixed with the last remnants of the old ramparts levelled after World War II. It is now 180 metres high, well planted with trees and shrubs and offers good walks and views.

Viale Monte Rosa Leave Piazzale Lotto by heading down Viale Monte Rosa towards the city. To the left, in Via Masaccio, is the church of San Siro alla Vepra. The area around the church was used in the twelfth-century by Milanese who had been expelled from the city by Barbarossa in 1162. Although dating originally from the ninth-century, the church was rebuilt in the mid-fifteenth only to be beheaded in the eighteenth-century when there was a spate of rebuilding in the area. Between the wars it was cleverly reconstructed and is now the headquarters of the Sisters of the Immaculate Conception. Inside, the church has some interesting frescoes and a Holy Water container made from an old Roman tomb, the sculpted children's heads suggesting it was made for a child.

One of Milan's newer museums can be visited a little further down Viale Monte Rosa. Take Via Tempesta, the next turning on the right, and go first right again into Via Mose Bianchi. At No.94 is the Museum of the Far East and of Ethnography. The museum is also occasionally known as the Museo PIME from the initial letters of the Pontificio Instituto Missioni Estere, the missionary body responsible for the collection. The collection

The Giuseppe Meazza Stadium, San Siro

represents years of voyages by missionaries to Asia, Oceania and Africa, but chiefly contains items from the Far Eastern countries of China, Japan, Burma and India.

Go down Viale Monte Rosa, to reach on the left, the Fiera Campionaria, Milan's trade exhibition site. From the outside the market area is impressive. From the inside it is even more impressive, but you will only see this if your visit coincides with an exhibition as the fair is only open at such times. The tourist office will be able to supply a list of exhibitions and their dates.

From the front entrance of the Fiera, on its southern side, where Via Spinola and Via Senofonte meet, it is a short step to the delightful Piazza Giulio Cesare. Here there is a fine fountain and a quiet seat, in fact everything, except a cup of coffee. Away from the Fiera and the fountain, off Piazza Buonarroti, is the musicians' rest home founded by Giuseppe Verdi to provide for the old age of musicians, the composer maintaining the home from his own pocket. Even the house itself, built in 1899 in Neo-Gothic style, was paid for from Verdi's royalties.

Both Verdi and his wife are buried here, their crypt being the work of Ludovico Pogliaghi, who was also responsible for the

**Piazza Giulio Cesare and
Fiera Campionaria**

bronze central door of the Duomo. Outside the house, in the small piazza in which it stands, is a fine memorial to the composer by Enrico Butti. In the statue Verdi is shown listening, while the relief sculptures at his feet represent melody, serenity, poetry and hatred, the four main elements of any opera.

Porta Garibaldi North of Parco Sempione, the driver who has emerged into the light from the Motorail terminal at Porta Garibaldi station usually finds himself confronted by a bunch of early-morning Milanese drivers and the sight of an awesome frontage, the Monumental Cemetery. Except in Paris, where Père Lechaise has become a spot on the tourist round, the cemeteries of most major cites are not a place to go. Milan is no exception. The specifically interested might look for the tombs of many of Italy's leading artists, some might admire the impressive architecture, but most will visit Villa Simonetta instead.

The villa is close to the cemetery, in Via Stilicone, that continues Via Messina, the road that runs up the cemetery's left – out of town side. It was built by one of Ludovico il Moro's officials and is the last remaining Renaissance country villa to be found in the city. The solid rather than delightful villa has an elegant façade with a three-

tiered columned loggia, but less graceful wings. After Ludovico's official had died it passed to the family Simonetta, but fell on hard times, eventually becoming a cholera hospital and then falling into disrepair before being further damaged by the bombs of 1943. Today it is nearing the completion of a methodical rebuilding.

Visitors should be wary of a story that is told to explain a remarkable echo at the villa. The story maintains that the echo can only really be heard when the word 'love' is spoken, the word being repeated up to thirty times. This, it continues is because the echo is not an echo at all but the ghost of one of the lovers of Celia Simonetta who brought young men to the villa, seduced them and then had them strangled by a faithful retainer.

North-west from Porta Garibaldi, a fine open square that can also be comfortably reached from the Central Station. North from the piazza runs Via Vassallo, to the left of which – but actually reached from Via Mirabello which is reached from either Via Bersezio and Via Colautti, both of which go left off Via Vassallo – is Villa Mirabello.

The villa dates from Visconti times, but was much reworked when it was bought by the Florentine banker Pigello Portinari who was responsible for the wonderful Portinari chapel in Sant' Eustorgio. Today the fine, courtyarded villa is the headquarters for a society looking after blinded ex-servicemen.

Some way north of Villa Mirabello is the Bicocca degli Arcimboldi, the very inappropriately named hovel of the Arcimboldis. This noble family built their country house in the late fifteenth-century but it became a focal point in a battle fought in 1522 at which the Milanese, supported by Spanish and German troops, defeated an army of French, Swiss and Venetian soldiers. It is said that even today the French have an expression, *C'est une bicoque*, for something that is bound to fail, so total was the defeat. The villa was badly damaged in the battle and became ruinous, perhaps acquiring its new name, and eventually became a farmhouse. Today it has been carefully restored and is a fine place, cream with terracotta window arches, and standing in an Italianate garden.

Out of the City With modern transport virtually anywhere in northern Italy is within long day-trip distance of Milan. Even Venice and Florence are only a couple of hours or so by fast efficient trains leaving from the Central Station. Here, however, we assume that you will not want to spend more than an hour or so on a train or behind the wheel of a car.

Monza and Gorgonzola Close to Milan the main tourist attractions are the city of Monza and the village of Gorgonzola. The first is comfortably reached by car; take the SS36 northward – or join it off the A4 taken eastwards, towards Venice (Venezia) – and then go off it to the city. Trains from Porta Garibaldi or the Central station reach Monza in about 15 minutes.

Monza is a small town famous for its autodrome where the Italian Grand Prix is usually staged. The autodrome is at the centre of a large and excellent park laid out in the early nineteenth century by Eugenio di Beuharnais. The park has a good camping site and is of interest to the motor-racing fan, because the autodrome is open to the public. For a few thousand lire the enthusiast can take his car on to the track and hurl it, and himself, around the circuit.

Less exciting, but also less dangerous, is a visit to the cathedral. This thirteenth-century Gothic Duomo is built on the site of a sixth-century church of Theodolinda, Queen of Lombardy, who was given a True Nail by Pope Gregory III for her act of converting the Lombards to Christianity. The Nail was beaten into a strip that formed the inner band of the *Corona Ferrea*, the Iron Crown that for a thousand years was used to crown the kings of the states of Italy. Both Charlemagne and Napoleon were crowned with it. Today the crown is held in Monza Cathedral, in the chapel of Queen Theodolinda, but is not always on show. Visitors specifically interested in seeing the crown should check in advance with the Monza Tourist Office at the Palazzo Communale (Tel: (039) 323222).

The Duomo also has a fine museum in which are a gold Evangelarium of Theodolinda and a sixth-century Byzantine cross once owned by Adaloaldo, a son of Theodolinda. Here too is a masterpiece of early Lombardian art, a gold hen with seven chicks, a piece whose age and purpose are still disputed by experts.

The Colleoni Chapel, Bergamo

Elsewhere in the town visitors should see the Villa Reale, a magnificent Neo-Classical building, although the *palazzo* is so large that to talk of a single building is to wildly understate the place. It was built by Piermarini for Ferdinand, Archduke of Austria, and houses a fine art gallery.

Gorgonzola is best reached by road; take the SS11 going east from the city, or from the Viale Palmanova exit on the Tangentiale. Gorgonzola is, in fact, little more than a village and is of real interest only for the cheese that takes its name.

Bergamo, reached off the A4 Venice (Venezia) *autostrada* – take the Bergamo exit – or by train in about 50 minutes from either Porta Garibaldi or Central stations, is almost worth a book of its own. The upper city is virtually traffic-free and this, together with its relative inaccessibility – it still lies within its Medieval walls and is reached by funicula – means it has maintained almost complete its Renaissance appearance. Many believe that Siena is the finest of all Italian medieval towns, but Bergamo, although smaller, must run it a very close race.

At the centre of the upper city, Bergamo Alta, is the Piazza Vecchio in which the Palazzo della Ragione is outstanding for its sheer beauty. Close to the Piazza is the Duomo with a fine dome, and the church of Santa Maria Maggiore; on the outside of this the Colleoni Chapel is a glorious addition, a masterpiece by the architect Amadeo. Elsewhere, any walk through the narrow, uneven streets of the city is bound to please.

Como The city of Como lies on the lake of the same name. The city can be reached by *autostrada* – take the A8 towards Varese/Como and branch off on the A9 to Como – or by train. Trains leave from the Central Station, and take about an hour, or from the station of the Ferrovie Nord in Piazza Cadorna. This railway is a private line, and its trains take about an hour to reach the city. Note that on the trains of the Ferrovie Nord return tickets are valid for one day only and, in any case, cost twice as much as singles.

In the early-twelfth century Como fought Milan for supremacy of the lake on which it stands, being heavily defeated in the Ten Years War. The city appealed to Barbarossa for help, both with its own rebuilding, and with the settling of old scores. This alliance led to Barbarossa's destruction of Milan and the formation of the

Isola Bella

Lombard League against him, and to Como's destruction of the Milanese-backed island city of Comacina. This destruction is 're-enacted' with fireworks every year on the Sunday after St John's Day, and the ceremony is one of the grandest of any in the area.

Como is a fine city with an excellent Duomo attached to an equally good *broletto*. The Piazza San Fedele is a lovely old square. The lake itself is beautiful, perhaps the most beautiful of all the big lakes, and even if you have a tight schedule you should try to take a boat trip. With good planning a trip by *aliscafo* (hydrofoil) to Bellagio, known as 'the jewel of the lake', and certainly one of the most exquisite towns in Italy, could be made.

Lake Maggiore, another of the great lakes, can also be easily visited. The A8 *autostrada* leads directly to Sesto Calende at the southern tip of the lake, a branch motorway reaching Varese. Trains run up the western shore of the lake, the line continuing by way of the Simplon tunnel to Switzerland, with Laveno on the

Isola Pescatori

225

eastern shore being reached by the Ferrovie Nord form Piazza Cadorna on a line that goes through Varese.

Lake Maggiore is famous for the Borromean Islands of Isola Bella, Isola Pescatori and Isola Madre. Bella is an astonishing place, built up from virtually nothing into a boat-shaped island topped with gardens. The interior decoration of the island's *palazzo* and the garden ornamentation are almost beyond description. The visitor must decide for himself whether it is delightful or completely over the top. Isola Madre, by contrast, is quiet and dignified, a superb garden around a fine mansion. The final island, Isola Pescatori, is quite different from each of the others, being still inhabited with fisherfolk. In many ways this is the best of the islands, the exchange of old-fashioned narrow streets for fine palaces being a fair one.

The islands are reached from Stresa, a justly famous lake resort with a range of very good hotels. From the town a cablecar reaches the top of the Mottarone, a mountain that offers views not only over the lake but over the Italian/Swiss Alps. Monte Rosa can be seen from here.

There is a railway station in Stresa, and also one in Arona near the southern tip of the lake. This was the town where San Carlo Borromeo was born and near which stands his monumental statue.

Isola Madre

Laveno, on the opposite shore from Stresa, is interesting for its cableway to the top of a local high point. The passenger carrier is a two-person open bucket of mesh to make the most of the view on the way up. It is an exciting ride, but not for those bothered by heights as a view of the drop is absolutely unavoidable. Elsewhere in the town do try to visit the studio of the sculptor Sergio Tapia Radic. This Chilean emigré is developing a reputation and following in Milan, and, indeed, throughout northern Italy, for his devotional and ceramic work. The studio is at 177 Via Labiena.

Varese is a modern city with amenities similar to those of Milan, but on a smaller scale.

En route to Lake Maggiore, whether you go by train or by *autostrada*, is Legnano. Those driving should leave the A8 at the Legnano exit. The town is famous for the battle fought here in 1176 when the cities of the Lombard League defeated the army of Barbarossa. The battle was turned by a group of soldiers under Alberto da Giussano who fought with a furious bravery. The group was known as the Compagnia della Morte, the Company of Death. The battlefield can be visited, it lies near the farmhouse of Mazzafame.

Today the town is more famous for the *Carroccio*, a horse race through the streets. There is also a fine church by Bramante, San Magno, which houses frescoes by several Lombardian artists including Bernardino Luini. The Visconti castle dates from the fifteenth century and houses an interesting 'culture' centre. The town museum should also be visited to see a precious Roman silver cup dating from the first, or perhaps second, century AD.

Lodi and Pavia South of Milan the attractions are further afield but there are exceptions. Lodi is a fine town, reached by car taking the Lodi exit off the A1 Piacenza/Bologna *autostrada*, or by train in about 50 minutes from the Central Station. The town has an ancient history, having been one of the members of the Lombard League. This was a rather odd change of heart since the town had been utterly destroyed by Milan and rebuilt – on a site several miles from that of the first town – by Barbarossa, the very man the League was formed to counter. Later the town was the site of a decisive battle, on 10 May 1796, between the forces of Napoleon and those of the Austrians. After defeating the Austrians, Napoleon entered Milan.

Lodi is set on the right bank of the Adda, and is grouped around the Piazza della Vittoria, a fine old square with fifteenth-century porticoes on all sides. The Piazza del Mercato is also very good. The Duomo is a fine building, but pride of place must go to the Sanctuario dell'Incoronato, now thought to be the finest Lombard Renaissance building in existence. The dome is superb, the loggias the very height of elegance. Elsewhere, the Ospedale Maggiore of Pellegrini is excellent.

Also to the south of Milan is Pavia, about 50 minutes by train from the Central Station, or reached by a branch motorway off the A7 Genoa *autostrada*.

Pavia was the capital of the earliest Lombardian kingdom in northern Italy and was also, for a short time, the capital of the Carolingian kingdom of Italy. In the battles between Barbarossa and Milan, Pavia supported the emperor, and was well rewarded after Milan's destruction. Later, these privileges were lost when the town became part of the Visconti Duchy.

In 1386 Gian Galeazzo Visconti pushed the protective wall of Pavia out nearly 8 kilometres (5 miles) north of the city, enclosing an area of parkland and finishing at the Certosa, built by him as a Carthusian monastery, it church designed to hold the Visconti tombs. Although the fortifications that once linked the Certosa to the town are gone, the monastic buildings are still there. The monastery was closed by Napoleon, but, since 1968, it has once more become the home of monks, in this case of the Cistercian Order.

Within the town of the Basilica of San Michele is in fine Romanesque style and dates from 1177, although it is on the site of an earlier Lombardian building. In earliest times, when Pavia was the capital, the Lombardian kings were crowned here. The Duomo is a later building, having been built, in part, by Bramante in Lombard Renaissance style.

Elsewhere, the Visconti castle is evidence of the need to hold the city after it had been annexed into the Duchy. The castle, the courtyard of which is superb, houses a fine historical museum and an art gallery.

Finally, be sure to see the Colegio Borromeo, built by one of San Carlo's favourite architects, Il Pellegrini, and with frescoes of the saint's life.

Vigevano South-west from Milan is the Piazza Ducale at Vigevano, among the finest Renaissance piazzas in Lombardy. It is widely thought to have been the work of Bramante, working on instructions from Ludovico il Moro. The nearby castle is the biggest in Italy. It is currently being restored, but you are allowed to visit those parts where work has already been completed.

You can also visit the town's Shoe Museum. With the reputation that Italy has for leatherwork in general, and shoes in particular, this is not such a bad idea, particularly as Vigevano is, and always has been, a shoe town. The museum is on the corner of Via Cesarea and Corso Cavour.

Part Four: **Further Information**

Southern Lake Como

Sundays and Rain Days This section is aimed chiefly at those who visit Milan with children. The city has enough 'inside things' available to keep adults occupied for days, but children can be more demanding.

If the weather is good, the Milan parks are the places to go. The narrow gauge railway in the public gardens, and the zoo in the same park are tailor-made, but the chief advantage is the space. The public gardens, Parco Sempione, the gardens of the Guastalla and the Rotonda have space enough to absorb hours. And in all of those parks there are very precise boundaries so that children and traffic do not mix.

Further afield, the Idroscalo is superb if your children love water. Close to it, and also to the Saini sports centre, in Strada Rivoltana, there is one of the two large Milanese Luna parks, amusement parks with the usual range of rides and games. The other park is in Viale Liberazione and the adjacent park here is where any visiting circuses will be found.

Further afield again, at Rivolta d'Abba on the SS11 from Milan to Brescia, there is a Prehistoric Park (closed on Tuesdays), with over 100 hectares (about 250 acres) of parkland with full-size models of dinosaurs in metal and plastic. There is also a very good restaurant here.

Off the A4 *autostrada* – use the Capriate exit – east of the city at Capriate San Gervasio there is a scale model of Italy, complete with scale models of the more important sites and monuments.

Further off again, a very long day will take you to the southern tip of Lake Garda. Take the A4 towards Venezia (Venice) as for Capriate above, but continue to the Peschiera del Garda exit, about 130 kilometres (80 miles) from Milan. Near Peschiera is

San Lorenzo

San Nazaro Maggiore

**Opposite
Duomo roof**

Gardaland, a mini-Disneyland with numerous rides including a corkscrew roller-coaster. Also near the village is the Caneva Water Park, with a huge collection of water chutes and pools.

For rain days many of the above suggestions still apply, particularly those that take you away from Milan as the local weather tends to be just that – local. In the city, if the Luna Parks do not appeal, the sports centres and pools are the best answer. For older children the hands-on exhibits at the National Museum of Science and Technology, the Aquarium and the Planetarium are very worthwhile.

Milan on a Time Budget For those with little time to spare the catalogue of sites worth a moment of your time will have seemed daunting, but, as with all cities, the list of the sites that absolutely must not be missed is much shorter.

234

Aware of this, the city has laid out a red line route – and I do literally mean 'laid out'; it is a red line on the pavement – that is recommended as the ultimate one-day tour of the major sites of Milan. The route, *Il filo rosso*, starts in Piazza della Scala with the Leonardo statue, La Scala and Palazzo Marino, then moves up Via Manzoni passing the Poldi-Pezzoli, enters Via Morone to see Manzoni's House, continuing through the Piazza Belgioioso. The line then takes Via San Andrea to reach the shopping area of Via Montenapoleone and Via della Spiga, then continues to the Arches of Porta Nuova. It takes Via Palestro past the public gardens, seeing Villa Reale, and then passes the fine *palazzos* of the Corso Venezia.

From San Babila, *Il filo rosso* goes along Via Durini and Via Festa del Perdono to reach Largo Richini and Ca'Grande. Going up Corso di Porta Romana and then through Piazza Velasca, the route reaches Via Mazzini and follows it to Piazza del Duomo. From the piazza it goes along Via Mercanti, passing Piazza dei Mercanti, to the Cordusio, continuing down Via Dante to see the Castle from Largo Cairoli. It goes along Via Cusani, then left past Santa Maria del Carmine.

The Red Line now takes you up Via Madonna to Via Fiori Chiari, right along it and then right again into Via Brera. Via Brera and Via Verdi beyond lead back to the Piazza della Scala.

The Red Line route has great merit. It visits the Piazza del Duomo and Piazza della Scala; it sees the Poldi-Pezzoli and the Brera; it visits Ca' Grande, one or two of the better churches – San Nazaro and Santa Maria del Carmine to be specific; and it sees the castle, if only from across a square.

What it does not see, and what it misses, are as important as what it does not miss – Santa Maria delle Grazie, Sant' Eustorgio and Sant' Ambrogio. It misses the frescoes of San Maurizio and the museum of the castle. It also misses green Milan for, although the Red Line walks past the public gardens, it does not go through them. It is an excellent attempt at capturing the city in one day, but perhaps not a wholly successful one.

Where does that leave the time-limited traveller? There are two alternatives. The first is to choose the best sites by period from the following list ; the second is to try to capture the very best, without regard for whether that adequately covers the spectrum of what the city has to offer.

Leonardo, Piazza della Scala

Roman Milan

Columns of San Lorenzo

Towers of Monastero Maggiore

Archaeological Museum

Early Christian Milan

Older parts of San Lorenzo

Older parts of San Simplicano

Older parts of San Nazaro

Romanesque Milan

(Ninth to Thirteenth-Centuries)

Basilica of Sant' Ambrogio

Museum of Sant' Ambrogio

Basilica of Sant' Eustorgio

Palazzo della Regione in Piazza dei Mercanti

Church of San Babila

Ducal Milan

(Fourteenth to mid-Sixteenth-Centuries)

Duomo

Church of Santa Maria delle Grazie

Leonardo da Vinci's *Last Supper*

Sforza Castle

Ospedale Maggiore (Ca' Grande)

Church of Santa Maria Miracoli presso San Celso

Frescoes of San Maurizio

Church of Santa Maria presso San Satiro

Church of San Gottardo

Palazzo Fontana-Silvestri

Palazzo Arcivescovile

Baroque Milan

(Mid-Sixteenth to early Eighteenth-Centuries)

Palazzo di Brera

Church of San Marco

Palazzo delle Scuolo Palatine

Palazzo Marino

Church of Santa Maria della Passione

Palazzo del Senato

Rococo Milan

(early to late Eighteenth-Century)

Palazzo Litta (Corso Magenta)

Opposite
Sforza Castle

Rotunda di Via Besana
Palazzo Dugnani

Neo-Classical Milan

(Late Eighteenth to mid-Nineteenth-Centuries)
Villa Reale
Palazzo Reale
Theatre of La Scala
Palazzo Belgioioso
Church of San Giorgio al Palazzo
Palazzo Melzi di Cusano

Nineteenth-Century Milan

Casa Manzoni
Galleria Vittorio Emanuele II

Early Twentieth-Century Milan

Palazzo Castiglioni
Central Station

Late Twentieth-Century Milan

Fiera Campionara
Pirelli Tower
Stadium Giuseppe Meazza (San Siro Football Stadium)

Milan in a Few Days Personal taste aside, you should attempt to see the Duomo – and preferably Milan from its roof – Sant' Ambrogio, the church of Santa Maria delle Grazie and the Sforza Castle, together with spending time in Piazza dei Mercanti (perhaps for lunch), and Piazza della Scala. If these visits include the Pietà Rondannini of Michelangelo in the Museum of the Castle and the *Last Supper* of Leonardo, I believe you will have done justice to the city.

If you have a second day, include Sant' Eustorgio, San Maurizio if it is open (and San Giorgio al Palazzo if it is not) and a restful hour in either the public gardens of the Parco Sempione. The visitor should do a little walking too, so that one of the better *palazzo*s can be seen – *Palazzo Fontana Silvestri* perhaps – the walk to include a look at Ca'Grande. Finally, one of the museums should be visited. Which one will depend on personal choice – the Ambrosiana with its Caravaggio and Leonardo portrait, Poldi-Pezzoli with the Pollaiolo profile, the Brera with the Mantegna *Cristo Morto*, Villa Reale's modern art, Palazzo Reale's

San Maurizio

contemporary work, or the Leonardo gallery in the Museum of Science and Technology.

If your visit extends to a third day, another of the museums can be 'done', as can some of the better 'minor' churches and 'lesser' *palazzo*s. Santa Mari Miracoli presso San Celso would be a

241

Palazzo Arcivescovile

good choice, together with Santa Maria presso San Satiro and San Lorenzo. The *palazzi*s will include Castiglioni and Melzi di Cusano, while time will also be available to include the Rotonda di Via Besana.

If your Milanese trip extends to one week, all the trips described here should be possible, although of course, it is rather dependent on how much time you spend inside each museum and church. One afternoon I was determined to do several of those things that had always been left out because of lack of time. That afternoon San Maurizio was open. Nothing else was done.

Entertainment Apart from La Scala, Milan has several other theatres; the tourist office will be able to let you have a programme for each of them. In addition there are several cinemas.

There are a variety of nightclubs, discos and piano bars, although to give a list is hardly likely to be much help. By the time you have reached the city the scene will have moved on. Some of those that appear to have withstood the test of time are *Champagneria* at No.1 Via Clerici (Tel: 800862, closed Sundays), and *Nepentha* in Piazza Diaz (Tel: 804837, closed Sundays). These

242

are both very exclusive clubs where the excellent ambience will cost you dear. Cheaper nightclubs are *William's* at No. 71 Foro Buonaparte (Tel: 877218, closed on Christmas Day!!), *Top Town* at No. 5 Via Paolo da Cannobio (Tel: 806151, closed Sundays, and *Paradise* in Piazza Velasca (Tel: 8050879), closed Sundays).

Piano bars are quieter, more intimate spots, the place for couples who want to be together with other people – if you see what I mean. They have soft lights and really do have pianos to offer soft music. Try *Manhattan* at No. 3 Via Verri (Tel: 793566, closed Sundays), *Tornavento* at No. 36 Alzaia Naviglio Grande (Tel: 8390068, closed Sunday), and *Brellin* at the corner of No.14 Alzaia Naviglio Grande (Tel: 8351351, closed Sunday).

Sports Milan has some of the finest sports facilities in Italy, both for the spectator and the competitor. For more details of the sports-watching complex of San Siro, *see* pages 215-216. For those wanting to take part in sport themselves during their visit, the list is almost endless.

The main sports centre in the city is the Saini at no. 136 Via Corelli (on bus route 38). The centre offers two football fields, a hockey field, a baseball square, four gyms (each fully equipped), three swimming pools, twelve tennis courts, a running track, two skating rinks and a plastic Nordic ski track.

In addition to the Saini there are about twenty other sport centres. If sport is what you are after, ask for a list at the Tourist Office.

As well as the sports centres there are other facilities. *Bocce*, Italian bowls, is practised in nearly 100 separate areas. There are four ten-pin bowling alleys. Canoeing and sailing are to be found at the Idroscalo. There in a fencing club. There are several golf courses within easy reach, together with a 9-hole course and several putting practice greens within the city. There are nearly 20 swimming pools, some of them open-air in addition to those of the Idroscalo and the Laghetto Redecesio (*see* page 195).

Photography There are an increasing number of fast photo developers in the city – look for the signs Quick Foto, Un'ora Foto or similar.

On the photography side, you will soon learn that taking photos in Milan is a question of shooting through the tram wires. In addition, you will find that the very deep shadows in some streets will throw out the exposure of average metering TTL cameras.

Theatre of La Scala

243

**Palazzo Reale – Sunday
shrub/flower market**

Language Guide

A Note on Pronounciation Italian is a straightforward language, in pronunciation terms, as all the letters in any word are pronounced and are always pronounced the same way. There is rarely emphasis on individual syllables as there is in English, Italian giving equal weight to all syllables. Thus *Reno*, a town on the eastern shore of Lake Maggiore is pronounced *Wren-o*, whereas the expectation of the English traveller would render it as *Ree-no*.

Some letters are pronounced differently from their rendering in English, however:

c before e or i is pronounced ch, e.g. dolce = dole chay, cinque = chin kway elsewhere c is pronounced as k

ch is pronounced k

g before e or i is pronounced j, elsewhere g is pronounced as a hard g

gh is pronounced as a hard g

gl is pronounced ly

gn is pronounced ne

he is silent

sc before e or i is pronounced sh, elsewhere sc is pronounced sk

z and zz is usually pronounced ts, though it is occasionally pronounced ds

A short Italian-English Dictionary In a book of this nature it is impossible to give a comprehensive language guide, but a few phrases that allow the visitor to move around the city with greater ease would seem appropriate. Below are some useful phrases and words that should help.

Good Morning	Buongiorno
Good Eevening	Buona Sera
Good Night	Buona Notte
Good-bye	Arrivederci
Bye, so long etc.	Ciao
Yes	Si
No	No
Please	Per favore
Thank you	Grazie

That's alright	Va bene
You're welcome, OK etc.	Prego
Where is ...?	Dov'é ...?
Where do I find ...?	Dove si trove ...?
I'm looking for ...	Cerco ...
Can I have ...?	Posso avere ...?
Is it ...?	E ...?
When ?	Quando ?
What ?	Che cosa ?
How much ?	Quanta costa ?
Can you tell me ... ?	Puo dirmi ... ?
I would like ...	Vorrei ...
Where is the nearest ... ?	Dov'é ... piú vicini ?
(I'm sorry) I don't understand	(Mi dispiace) non capisco
Do you speak English ?	Parla Inglese
Is there anyone here who speaks English ?	C'é qualcuno qui che parla inglese ?
open/closed	aperto/chiuso
hot/cold	caldo/freddo
big/small	grande/piccolo
good/bad	buono/cattivo
currency exchange	cambio

0	zero	6	sei
1	uno	7	sette
2	due	8	otto
3	tre	9	nove
4	quattro	10	dieci
5	cinque	100	cento
1000	mille (but 2000 – duemila, 5000 – cinquemila etc.)		
1st	primo	2nd	secondo
3rd	terzo		

Sunday	Domenica
Monday	Lunedi
Tuesday	Martedi
Wednesday	Mercoledi
Thursday	Giovedi
Friday	Venerdi
Saturday	Sabato

In the Hotel

a room	una camera
two, three rooms	due, tre camere
with bathroom	con bagno
with shower	con doccia
with toilet	con gabinetto
... days	... giorni
one week	una settimana

In Italian hotels breakfast is very rarely included in the price, though it will usually be available (at a price). Check whether the price is *colazione incluso*. If not, then check the price of the hotel breakfast: it is probably cheaper to eat in a local bar.

Motoring

Use headlights in tunnel	Ascendere i fari in galleria
Keep right (left)	Accostre a destra (sinistra)
Walk (at pedestrian crossings)	Avanti
No parking	Divieto di sosta (occasionally sosta vietata)
Road works	Lavori in corso
Danger	Pericolo
Reduce speed	Rallentare
Pedestrian zone	Zona pedonale
One way	Senso unico
No entry	Senso vietato
No through road	Vicola cicco

Milan Index